DYSCALCULIA

ACTION PLANS FOR SUCCESSFUL LEARNING IN MATHEMATICS

Glynis Hannell

 David Fulton Publishers

David Fulton Publishers
2 Park Square, Milton Park, Abingdon, Oxon OX14 4RN

270 Madison Avenue, New York, NY 10016

David Fulton Publishers is an imprint of the Taylor & Francis Group, an informa business

Copyright © Glynis Hannell 2005

British Library Cataloguing in Publication Data
A catalogue record for this book is available from the British Library.

ISBN: 1 84312 387 8

Typeset by Servis Filmsetting Ltd, Manchester

CONTENTS

SECTION ONE: INTRODUCTION TO DYSCALCULIA

Chapter 1 Understanding dyscalculia	**2**
What is dyscalculia?	2
How common is dyscalculia?	3
Are dyscalculia and dyslexia the same thing?	3
What causes dyscalculia?	4
The brain and mathematics	4
Dyscalculia and language	5
Dyscalculia and visuospatial skills	8
Dyscalculia and memory	11
Dyscalculia and attitudinal and emotional factors	13
Identifying pupils with dyscalculia	14

SECTION TWO: EFFECTIVE TEACHING – EFFECTIVE LEARNING

Chapter 2 The biological basis of learning	**18**
How does the brain 'learn'?	18
Action plans for successful learning	23
Chapter 3 Making mathematical connections	**24**
Seeing the world through mathematical eyes	24
Making connection with what the child already knows	26
Learning has to make sense and fit into the big picture	26
Learning is better if it occurs in multiple contexts	27
Making sense of manipulatives	28
Generalising learning	29
Parents are important teachers: help them to make the connections	29
Understanding the purpose of mathematics	30
Action plans for successful learning	31

Chapter 4   Assessment   **35**
What is valued?   35
What does competence look like?   35
Working it out your own way   36
Let the errors tell the story   37
Don't get caught not knowing   38
Pupils who evaluate their own learning know what counts   38
Action plans for successful learning   39

Chapter 5   Individual differences and mathematics   **40**
Matching teaching style to learning style   40
Using the theory of multiple intelligences   41
Verbal-linguistic intelligence   42
Interpersonal intelligence   42
Kinesthetic intelligence   43
Naturalist intelligence   43
Musical, rhythmic intelligence   44
Intra-personal intelligence   44
Spatial intelligence   45
Logical-mathematical intelligence   46
Aesthetic intelligence   47
Action plans for successful learning   47

Chapter 6   Confidence and mathematics   **48**
Effective learning environments foster self-confidence   48
Confidence grows from the belief that you can succeed   49
Anxiety disrupts thinking   49
Action plans for successful learning   50

SECTION THREE: UNDERSTANDING THE NUMBER SYSTEM

Chapter 7   Introduction to understanding the number system **54**
Dyscalculia and the number system   54

Chapter 8   Counting   **57**
Saying the correct sequence   57
Using 1:1 correspondence when counting   58
Action plans for successful learning   58

Using counting skills flexibly   59
Action plans for successful learning   59
Classification and counting   61
Action plans for successful learning   61
Counting in any order, counting each item once   62
Action plans for successful learning   63

Chapter 9   Understanding the base 10 system   **64**
Base 10 and dyscalculia   64
Action plans for successful learning   65

Chapter 10   Understanding place value in written numbers   **68**
Place value and dyscalculia   68
Action plans for successful learning   69

Chapter 11   Composition and decomposition of numbers   **72**
Dyscalculia and composition and decomposition of numbers   72
Action plans for successful learning   73

Chapter 12   Order of magnitude of numbers and their relationship with each other   **76**
Order of magnitude and dyscalculia   76
Action plans for successful learning   78

SECTION FOUR: UNDERSTANDING OPERATIONS

Chapter 13   Dyscalculia and operations   **82**

Chapter 14   Understanding algorithms   **84**
Action plans for successful learning   85

Chapter 15   Addition   **89**
Strategies   90
Action plans for successful learning   91
Using vertical setting out   94
Action plans for successful learning   96

Chapter 16   Subtraction   **98**
Strategies   98

Action plans for successful learning   99
Using vertical setting out   100
Action plans for successful learning   101

Chapter 17 Multiplication   **103**
Action plans for successful learning   103

Chapter 18 Division   **106**
Action plans for successful learning   107

Chapter 19 Learning number facts   **109**
Action plans for successful learning   109

SECTION FIVE: MEASUREMENT AND RATIONAL NUMBERS

Chapter 20 Measurement   **114**
Dyscalculia and measurement   114
Action plans for successful learning   116

Chapter 21 Rational numbers   **118**
Dyscalculia and rational numbers   118
Action plans for successful learning   119

SECTION SIX: TEACHER RESOURCES

Parent information sheets
Parent Information Sheet: At home with maths   124
Parent Information Sheet: Maths on the move   127
Parent Information Sheet: At home with telling the time   130

Questionnaires
What I think about maths (Pupil questionnaire)   133
Your child and maths (Parent questionnaire)   134

References and bibliography   **136**

INTRODUCTION TO DYSCALCULIA

Literacy difficulties account for over 90% of the research literature on learning disorders, and yet in every classroom there are children struggling with mathematics and teachers trying to work out the best way to assist them. This book outlines the essentials of the condition called dyscalculia and offers numerous practical ways in which these difficulties can be addressed.

Chapter 1
UNDERSTANDING DYSCALCULIA

WHAT IS DYSCALCULIA?

The term 'dyscalculia' is used to describe specific difficulties with mathematics. In many ways it is the mathematical equivalent of dyslexia, which is a specific difficulty with literacy.

Pupils with dyscalculia seem to be just as intelligent as their peers. They have been taught in the same way and engaged in the same mathematical activities – and yet they encounter distinct difficulties in mastering the basics of mathematical thinking. As a result they often fail to acquire the essential concepts that underpin skills in performing mathematical procedures.

The disorder is also sometimes referred to as 'developmental dyscalculia', indicating that it is a developmental problem, as distinct from a difficulty that has been acquired through accident, illness, poor teaching or other adverse circumstances.

Although there is general agreement that some individual pupils do, quite clearly, have specific and sometimes severe difficulties with mathematics, there is also considerable professional debate about the precise nature of dyscalculia, its extent and its precise causes.

The word 'dyscalculia' means literally a 'disorder in calculation'. The Department for Education and Skills defines developmental dyscalculia as 'a condition that affects the ability to acquire arithmetical skills. Dyscalculic learners may have difficulty understanding simple number concepts, lack an intuitive grasp of numbers and have problems learning number facts and procedures.'

In the USA the National Center for Learning Disabilities defines dyscalculia as 'a wide range of life long learning disabilities involving math. There is no single form of math disability, and difficulties vary from person to person and affect people differently in school and throughout life.'

Mathematics is a complex curriculum area. It requires a wide range of skills across several quite distinct domains, such as perceptual reasoning, verbal reasoning, counting and calculating. Geary (2004) points out that many pupils with dyscalculia can do very well indeed in some domains of the mathematics curriculum and yet have substantial difficulties in others, and therefore reminds us that achievement tests containing a range of mathematical tasks (such as arithmetic, geometry, problem solving and measurement) can be very misleading. Strengths in one area can easily cancel out weaknesses in others. This means, of course, that the overall score may be a very unreliable indicator of the pupil's mathematical ability.

Geary also points out that research has concentrated to a very large extent on difficulties with arithmetic and that other, important areas of mathematical ability have been, to a large extent, neglected by the researchers. However, in general it is true to say for the majority of pupils with dyscalculia the primary deficits are in arithmetic, calculation and the understanding of basic mathematical concepts.

HOW COMMON IS DYSCALCULIA?

There is general agreement that about 5–8% of pupils have dyscalculia (Geary, 2004). On average every class of 30 children will have two or three pupils who are affected by it.

Geary also comments that some pupils who do poorly in mathematics in one year may perform well in the next, reminding us that the quality of teaching in itself can either create or protect against learning difficulties in mathematics.

So in addition to the two or three pupils in your class with a true dyscalculia, you may also be working with other children with apparently similar difficulties but who have in fact acquired these through poor learning experiences in earlier years. However, such pupils should improve quickly once they are given appropriate instruction. Pupils with dyscalculia will need more intensive help, and will respond to this much more slowly.

ARE DYSCALCULIA AND DYSLEXIA THE SAME THING?

We know that there is considerable overlap between these two disorders: Butterworth and Yeo (2004) suggest that somewhere between 20 and 60% of pupils have both. Deficits in language and working memory may well create problems in the acquisition of both mathematics and literacy skills. However, the two disorders can also exist in isolation from each other.

It is fair to say that of the two disorders, dyslexia is usually more readily recognised and remedied, while mathematical difficulties often seem to go unnoticed. Perhaps this is because mathematics is seen as an intrinsically challenging subject, where it is more 'normal' and therefore acceptable to have difficulties.

WHAT CAUSES DYSCALCULIA?

We do know that there is a strong genetic influence on the development of mathematical skills. Just as we find one family where parents and children are all very capable mathematicians, we often identify another in which mathematical difficulties are very common.

Obviously, we must remember that environmental factors will play their part in the transmission of a talent for, or a difficulty in, mathematics. A family where parents are mathematically competent may be a very different learning environment to one in which parents are uncertain about basic mathematics themselves.

However, it is clear that the biological influences do play a significant role in dyscalculia. For instance, Shalev and Gross-Tur (2001) found that about 50% of the siblings of a pupil with dyscalculia can be expected to have it as well. Parents and siblings of a pupil with dyscalculia are ten times more likely to have dyscalculia than members of the general population.

THE BRAIN AND MATHEMATICS

Some pupils will be blessed with brains that seem purpose-built for mathematics. Other pupils may have dyscalculia and find mathematical thinking very difficult in comparison to other types of thinking and learning.

All learning and thinking develops through the evolution of specialised structures within the brain. Some of these structures are equipped to deal with the types of processes involved in mathematics. Between individuals there will naturally be differences in the efficiency with which these structures work. You will find much more information on the role that brain development plays in the acquisition of mathematics (and other learning) in Chapter 2.

It is generally agreed that mathematical competence depends on effective functioning of the pupil's

- language skills
- visuospatial skills
- memory.

As you will see as you read this book, successful mathematical thinking therefore often requires the efficient integration of several different types of learning and thinking.

DYSCALCULIA AND LANGUAGE

Many pupils with dyscalculia have significant difficulties with the language of mathematics.

Early language is the starting point for mathematical thinking

We know that language is a very important tool for the communication of information, questions and ideas. Much of a young child's understanding of mathematical concepts will be tightly bound up with their language development. They will learn about words and phrases such as *more, less, bigger, longer, twice, before, after, the same as, enough.* They will learn to count and name shapes, often before they start school.

Pupils with inadequate language skills may have general problems in their language skills development or they may have particular difficulty with the language related to mathematical concepts such as position, relationships and size: *The yesterday after tomorrow, It's less bigger than my one.*

Mathematical thinking will be more difficult without good language skills

Language is a very important vehicle for thinking. It is extremely difficult to deal with new ideas, understand abstract concepts, manipulate information and ideas, solve problems and remember previous learning without using appropriate language. If pupils do not have adequate language skills, their ability to handle some concepts and ideas will be reduced.

It is difficult to 'capture' concepts such as *double, bigger than, twice as much as, two triangles and a circle* or *two million people* if you cannot use words as labels; but with adequate external or internal language a child can represent not only objects but also actions and concepts, all essential elements in mathematical reasoning and learning.

Language is important as a way of carrying thinking forward: *I'll have to work out how many people there were and then I can divide that number.* Language also helps to link new ideas with ones already mastered: *This is a ten, so I think that I can break it up to make more ones … yes that will work, now I have got 13 ones.*

Language is also very important in helping to handle sequences and maintain the order of information or a procedure: *First I have to do write down the three, and then I have to carry the four.* Sequenced language may be particularly difficult for children with dyscalculia.

Children with dyscalculia may not understand the language they recite

Some pupils with dyscalculia have particular difficulty in linking the actions that they are supposed to perform with meaningful language. All too often they have learned a script that is, essentially a meaningless incantation – *Two plus two eagles four, Six take two you can't do, so borrow a ten* – when they have no idea what all of this actually means.

Children with dyscalculia may not use internal language to help with mathematics

Pupils with mathematics learning difficulties often cannot, or do not, use their own internal language to manage the mathematical tasks they are attempting (Garnett, 1998). They may imitate actions that they see their teachers or peers demonstrate, but fail to connect with the internal language that is supposed to accompany the process being taught.

> *Sam was having a lot of difficulties with his basic addition. He was asked to show the teacher what he was doing.*
>
> *He looked at the sheet of numbers and then looked away. He half closed his eyes and touch counted his fingers. He then put down a number and repeated the process again for the next item.*
>
> *Asked what he had just done, he said,* I counted like Sarah does.
>
> *Sam was merely copying what he observed of Sarah's behaviour and had not understood the internal language that was taking place when Sarah worked out the answer. Because he was working with numbers less than ten, he sometimes got the correct answer by chance.*

Mathematics has its own unique language

Mathematics has a language all of its own: sometimes it uses words or written symbols that are unique and need to be learned. For instance, *tens, subtract, addend, multiplication* and *algorithm* are seldom heard outside the mathematics classroom.

Other words may be familiar to the children, but are used in quite a different context: *olden times/times tables, take away food/take away sums, stereo unit/tens and units.*

For pupils who may be having trouble with their first language, mathematical language can cause a lot of anxiety and frustration. What does *equals* mean to the child who thinks of it as *eagles*? What is the difference between *What is the time? I make it ten to two* and *What is ten times two?*

> *Josh was asked to count to ten. Then he was told,* Now do it backwards. *He got off his chair and walked backwards while repeating the one to ten counting sequence!*

Language helps to monitor thinking and learning

Language is also very important in the way in which we monitor our own thinking and learning. Very young children generally do not demonstrate capacity to think about their own thinking (metacognition).

Pupils with learning difficulties such as dyscalculia may have difficulty in monitoring their own learning through internal, language-related thinking. As a result they may often not ask for help, because they cannot put into words what it is they do not know or understand.

> How do I know what it is I don't know? All I know is that I just don't get it!
> *Frank, 14*

Throughout this book you will find further discussion, and many examples, of the importance of language skills in all areas of mathematics.

DYSCALCULIA AND VISUOSPATIAL SKILLS

Pupils with dyscalculia may not use visual images effectively and may find reasoning that depends on holistic, spatial reasoning difficult to understand

Many mathematical concepts are usually most readily understood if they can be associated with a visual image.

10 11 12 13 14 15 16 17 18 19 20 21 22 23 24 25 26 27 28 29 30

This visual image usually helps children to understand the relationship of the numbers, by judging positions relative to each other and to the sequence of numbers as a whole: *20 is half way between 10 and 30, 6 is before 10 but after 5, Numbers ending in 0 occur at regular intervals, There is a pattern in the way that the numbers repeat themselves.*

However, some pupils with dyscalculia find this type of visual imagery difficult to work with and understand. When asked to locate a number on the number line they may search up and down in a random way, and demonstrate little awareness of where they might expect to find the number. They may find it difficult to judge distances between numbers or find the midpoint of the line.

A pupil with dyscalculia may not readily notice that a visual sequence such as *20, 21, 22, 23, 24, 25* follows a distinct visual and conceptual pattern. It may be difficult to develop an intuitive 'feel' for the order of magnitude of the numbers in the line. More particularly, they may find it very difficult to visualise the line and work from it when it is not actually in view.

Teaching concepts such as fractions often use visuospatial teaching aids such as diagrams of circles divided into halves, quarters or thirds. Some pupils with dyscalculia may find it so difficult to make sense of these diagrams that the concept of fractions (which might have been readily understood if presented linguistically) is lost to them.

Mental manipulation of images may be difficult for the pupil with dyscalculia

Rotating images mentally may be difficult for the pupil who has visuospatial difficulties. So symmetry, tessellation and geometry may all prove to be real challenges.

'Holding' a visual image and recording it accurately can be difficult too. This illustration shows what happened when a boy had to copy the number line down. He had to turn around to see the line and then turn back to record it in his book, and this process totally destabilised his sense of direction and his ability to retain the orientation of the numbers in the line.

εP, ϸP, ƨP, ϸP, ΓP, 8P, PP, 001

Measurement and understanding of space may be difficult for the pupil with dyscalculia

Measurement, space and shape do of course have a very direct link to visuospatial abilities.

For some young pupils with mathematics learning difficulties, even copying simple shapes can be very difficult. Look at how much trouble this 6-year-old had with copying the diagonal lines in this shape:

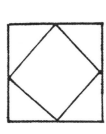 

We know he can draw straight lines because his rectangle/square is not too badly drawn, but drawing a straight line on the diagonal, and relating it to another line is just too hard.

Older pupils may have difficulties with accurate measurement and with grasping the concept of area, perimeter and volume.

Look at how this 9-year-old tried to record his measurement of a table with a 30 cm ruler. He has used a system of trying to count how many ruler lengths each side is.

But we can see he has not lifted and placed the ruler correctly so that he has ended up with an uneven number of 'rulers' on each side. He has not read the numbers on his ruler or calculated their totals correctly. Nor has he realised that two equal sides cannot measure 3 cm and 40 cm respectively.

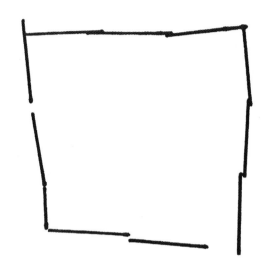

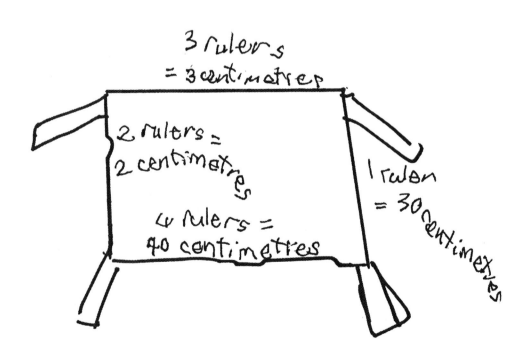

The setting out of working depends on good visuospatial skills

Placement of figures and symbols is an important part of working mathematically: it matters whether you work from left to right or in the opposite direction when you add tens and units, and it makes a difference if you try to take the top number from the bottom number in subtraction.

$$\begin{array}{r} 21 \\ -\ 19 \\ \hline 18 \end{array}$$

If you use scattered tally marks they are really hard to count accurately.

$$6 + 5 = 10$$

DYSCALCULIA AND MEMORY

It is clear that pupils with dyscalculia frequently have memory deficits (Wilson and Swanson, 2001; Gathercole and Pickering, 2000; Geary, 2004). The deficits may be in working memory (immediate memory that is used to store on-going, short-term information), or in long-term memory (where we store information for a period of time and then retrieve it).

Geary states, *Many children with MLD [mathematics learning disabilities] have difficulties in retrieving basic arithmetic facts from long term memory, a deficit that often does not improve.*

Wilson and Swanson (2001) showed that working memory deficits in both the verbal and visuospatial domains contribute to mathematics disabilities. In this book you will read more about the impact that deficits in working memory have in the various areas of mathematics that our pupils face both in school and in the world around them.

It has to be said that memory difficulties are particularly apparent when the pupil lacks a solid conceptual understanding of the process that they are attempting. If, for example, you understand the process of long multiplication you are far less dependent on remembering the steps in the process. If you forget how to do it you can, with some time and application, work out what to do and proceed correctly, not because you have remembered what to do, but because you understand what to do and have been able to work out the correct procedure for yourself.

Working memory

One element of working memory is the language-based 'phonological loop', where words are held temporarily while they are part of a process (such as calculating a total).

Difficulties in working memory may mean that you have to depend on counting on your fingers or making tally marks to keep a hold of where you are and what you are doing when you are calculating. Poor working memory will make it hard to recite multiplication tables because you forget where you are in the sequence as you recite.

> *I did know nearly all the answers in mental, but I forgot the questions. The teacher went too fast and I got all mixed up.*
> Patrick, 10

Poor working memory in the visuospatial domain may mean that your 'visuospatial sketchpad' is unreliable. This in turn may mean that you import errors into your work, not because you do not understand what you are doing, but because you make mistakes when you copy your working out or transfer geometric forms from one place to another.

Long-term memory

Long-term memory deficits are usually very obvious in the child or adolescent with mathematical difficulties. Often the pupil can be seen carefully counting their fingers to reconstitute a number fact that they have failed to retrieve from their memory.

To be successful in basic mathematics you have to remember written symbols (such as $+$ and $\times$) and the processes that they represent. You also have to remember a large number of basic number facts such as $3 + 7 = 10$, $6 \times 6 = 36$, *double 12 is 24.* Good long-term memory is also required for accurate recall and the correct application of procedural rules.

> *You know that stuff about how you can't have more than a nine, does that apply to add ups?*
> *Rebecca, 8*

Lack of sound conceptual understanding compounds the deficits caused by poor memory. You will find more information about memory and suggestions for intervention to improve it throughout this book.

DYSCALCULIA AND ATTITUDINAL AND EMOTIONAL FACTORS

Did you know?

- 9-year-olds with dyscalculia have, on average, the same level of mathematics knowledge and understanding as a typical 6-year-old.
- 17-year-olds with dyscalculia have, on average, the same level of mathematics knowledge and understanding as a typical 10-year-old.
- Pupils with dyscalculia seem to reach a plateau at the end of primary school and may only make one more year of progress in mathematics throughout their secondary schooling.
- 35% of pupils with learning disabilities drop out of secondary school early.

(Levine, 2002)

Dyscalculia can have a dramatic impact on a pupil's mind set towards mathematics. Pupils who start off at school eager to learn may quickly become confused and frustrated by the difficulties that they encounter.

Math is to hard becase it is lots of numbrs and I can't do it

It is generally true that motivation and application are two very good barometers of a pupil's confidence in any subject area. Unwilling and unco-operative learners are very frequently found to lack the foundation skills that they need to participate successfully in the task that is set.

Mathematics does require clear thinking and steady concentration, and we know that anxiety can seriously disrupt these important elements of mathematics thinking. Because anxiety, frustration, confusion and failure so often disrupt motivation, any pupil who shows disinterest, poor behaviour or lack of application to mathematics tasks should be assumed to be experiencing difficulties completing what they are being asked to do.

Throughout this book you will find out more about motivation and dyscalculia.

IDENTIFYING PUPILS WITH DYSCALCULIA

There are a range of warning signs that a particular child or adolescent may have dyscalculia. Some of them are outlined here.

Slowness

- Slow to give answers to mathematics questions.
- Slow in working in comparison with others.

Reliance on tangible counting

- Has difficulties with mental calculation.
- Uses fingers to count simple totals.
- Uses tally marks where others use mental calculation.
- Uses the 'counts all' method instead of 'counting on' when using fingers or manipulatives for addition.
- Finds it difficult to estimate or give approximate answers.

Difficulties with the language of mathematics

- Finds it difficult to talk about mathematical processes.
- Does not ask questions, even when he or she evidently does not understand.
- Finds it difficult to generalise learning from one situation to another.
- Makes mistakes in interpreting word problems, and instead just 'number crunches' the numbers in the text.
- Gets mixed up with terms such as *equal to, larger than*.

Difficulties with memory for mathematics

- Finds it difficult to remember basic mathematics facts.
- Has trouble remembering what symbols such as + mean.
- Forgets previously mastered procedures very quickly.
- Has to recite the entire multiplication table to get to an answer such as $4 \times 6 = 24$.
- Works multiplication tables out by adding on as they recite.
- Finds mental mathematics difficult, forgets the questions before the answer can be worked out.

Difficulties with sequences

- Loses track when counting.
- Loses track when saying tables: *2 times 3 is 6, 3 times 3 is 9, 5 times 3 is* (adds on 3 to previous answer) *12.*
- Has difficulty remembering the steps in a multi-stage process.

Difficulties with position and spatial organisation

- Is confused about the difference between *21* and *12*, and uses them interchangeably.
- Mixes up + and ×.
- Puts numbers in the wrong place when redistributing or exchanging.
- Poor setting out of calculations and of work on a page.
- Scatters tally marks instead of organising them systematically.
- Unaware of the difference between $6 - 2$ and $2 - 6$, says *4* is the answer in both cases.
- Gets confused with division: *Is it 3 into 6, or 6 into 3?*
- In tens and units takes the smaller number from the larger, regardless of position.
- Finds rounding numbers difficult.
- Finds telling the time on an analogue clock difficult.
- Is easily overloaded by worksheets full of mathematics.
- Copies work inaccurately.

Reliance on imitation and rote learning instead of understanding

- Can 'do' sums mechanically but cannot explain the process.
- Sometimes uses the wrong working method such as treating a ten as a one (or vice versa) in exchanging or redistribution.

$$38$$
$$57$$
$$185$$

$$8 + 7 = 15$$
$$15 + 3 = 18$$

EFFECTIVE TEACHING – EFFECTIVE LEARNING

The following chapters look at the basic principles of effective learning. Designing effective teaching programmes is much easier if we understand what makes effective learning. It sounds obvious but it is surprising how often we forget this basic principle.

You will see that the basic principles of effective teaching and learning outlined here have been used extensively to underpin the practical teaching strategies that are detailed in the remaining pages of this book.

The book is about dyscalculia, but as you read you will see that many of the suggestions will work equally well in teaching mathematics to all pupils, whether or not they have learning difficulties.

Chapter 2
THE BIOLOGICAL BASIS OF LEARNING

Did you know?

- Learning changes the physical structure of the brain.
- These structural changes reconfigure the organisation and function of the brain.
- Different parts of the brain may be ready to learn at different times.

(National Research Council, 2002)

HOW DOES THE BRAIN 'LEARN'?

Brain cells are called neurons and there are at least 100 billion of them in the human brain (Nolte, 1988). Each neuron has a cell body and a tree-like structure of branches called dendrites. The dendrites from one cell connect with those from other cells at the synapses, and exchange information.

The synapses are a very important part of the learning process. Those that are frequently used become more complex and much more efficient at processing information. Those that are neglected fail to develop.

Synapses develop in two main ways. In the first few years of life a child produces many, many more synapses than will ever be used. Incoming experiences activate some synapses which develop increased connections with other neurons. Synapses that are not used are selectively lost.

The second way of development is through the addition of new synapses throughout life, through an 'on demand' process. If a new synapse is needed the brain will, within limits, create one!

Four groups of rats were studied. The first group had a month of challenging acrobatic activities as they learnt to transverse an elevated obstacle course, the second group of rats had compulsory exercise on a treadmill, the third group had unlimited access to an activity wheel, and a control group of 'cage potatoes' had no exercise at all. At the end of the month the acrobats were the stand out winners when synapses were counted. Learning created synapses, exercise alone did not!
National Research Council, 2000

But what, we might ask, do acrobatic rats have to do with children with dyscalculia? The basic principles are the same. Learning new skills successfully develops brain connections.

Every individual learner has a brain circuitry that varies in its aptitudes when compared with others. Pupils with dyscalculia generally have more difficulty than most in building at least some of the neurological systems required for calculation and skilled mathematical thinking.

Why can't Ben just sit down and do this new maths problem straight away?

Because he has never done anything like this before, his brain has not yet had a chance to get the appropriate synapses working together effectively.

Can a teacher help Ben to learn?

Yes, a good teacher will know the right exercises to get those new synapses developing as fast as possible. Ben's brain will need to build the synapses that process the basic skills needed for this new problem and then Ben will need extra synapses to deal with this particular type of problem.

If Anna practices, can she acquire the skills necessary to do this problem?

That depends on how close she is to being able to do this task. If her brain can already connect with what she is learning so that it makes sense to her, then yes, the synapses that she is using will get bigger and better the more that she practices.

If the task is too far out of her range then practice will not help, because she will not have the underlying synapses available to do the task. Instead she might be copying what her friend has done, or just imitating the teacher without knowing what she is doing.

Jack has been practising for nearly a week and he's nearly got it, can he try something else now?

No, you have not given Jack's brain circuitry enough time to set itself up. If he's 'nearly got it' then there's still building work and consolidation to be done in the synapses before we can say that Jack has learnt this properly.

Casey can do addition to ten, so can she try algebra next?

No. Casey's brain circuitry (like yours and mine) will only rewire itself in gradual stages. Synapses that can handle simple tasks will not be able to switch to hard tasks without further training.

How come Ted's sister is learning faster than him, even though he practises more?

Her brain circuitry is probably better suited to learning mathematics. Ted's brain may need to learn in smaller steps and have more practice than his sister's. If Ted has dyscalculia then you may find that some types of mathematical thinking are really difficult to wire up effectively, so Ted may need to use a calculator or a computer to help out.

Can't they just learn the times tables by heart and learn maths that way?

No. All that will happen is that their brains will develop little, mini circuits of synapses, just for reciting times tables. They still won't be able to use mathematical thinking properly.

Once they can do mathematics properly will they always be able to do it well?

Once they have really built up those synapses they will always be better at mathematics than they were (although they will need to keep practicing to keep their mathematical brain circuits in good shape).

Learning accumulates gradually as the brain structures develop

Learning is a gradual, accumulative biological process. It depends on the child having a range of experiences, of graded difficulty, that trigger the development of the underlying neurological connections. Like building up physical fitness, the process of building mathematical fitness is one of regular training, with gradual increments of difficulty and plenty of practice sessions. Although the brain is not a muscle, many of the same principles as for physical fitness apply when we are looking to optimise its learning.

The best learning occurs at the boundary between what the child can already do, and what they cannot yet do. Tasks that the pupil can do with just a little help will generate the best learning. The teacher will activate existing synapses and build up their strength and efficiency. New synapses may also be developed through structured learning experiences.

The technique called 'graduated prompting' is effective. The adult gives as much help as is needed and gradually fades out the prompts as the pupil picks up the idea for themselves. Tasks that yesterday needed adult assistance will become tasks that can be done unaided tomorrow. Without the benefit of adult prompting, the pupil may well still be stuck at the 'can't do' stage of learning.

What about right and left brain learners?

It is true that the two halves of the brain are specialised, with the left hemisphere usually dealing primarily with language-related, sequenced information processing, and the right brain being more commonly involved in spatial reasoning and 'whole picture' thinking. However, the brain is an extraordinarily complex organism, with many interconnecting and complementary systems. While the majority of us do have language located mainly in the left hemisphere and spatial reasoning in the right hemisphere, there are frequent exceptions to this pattern of 'wiring'.

Although the brain is in two, quite distinct, halves there is a complex and intricate system of interconnection between the functions of both hemispheres. While some of us may be predominantly left- or right-brain thinkers, we can generally use either style of thinking quite efficiently, depending on the demands of a particular situation. Sometimes the thinking is primarily right brain, sometimes left: but most often both thinking styles merge, each supplementing the other to maximise the efficiency of the thinking process.

Mathematics requires the integration of many aspects of thinking, sometimes making heavy demands on language skills, sometimes requiring spatial reasoning to take the lead. Many children with difficulties with mathematics will have deficits in language or in spatial reasoning. The verbal and visuospatial aspects of learning in pupils with dyscalculia are dealt with in more detail throughout this book.

Where do we start?

The brain develops building blocks in the synapses that are the foundation for later, more advanced learning. It is essential to start instruction at the level where the pupil has already developed a good basic understanding and where remaining uncertainties respond quickly to appropriate teaching. This helps the brain to continue to build up strong and efficient synapses.

Attempting to teach in a situation where the underlying synapses for the task are absent is certain to cause frustration and make both pupil and teacher feel discouraged.

Practice, practice, practice

> *It has been estimated that it takes a world-class chess player up to 100,000 hours of practice to acquire the skills needed to play at that level. And we can assume that the player started with a natural aptitude for the game!*

It cannot be emphasised enough that quality and volume of practice (on tasks that have an appropriate level of difficulty) are often the deciding factors in the pupil's progress in mathematical competence.

Many children with dyscalculia work slowly and often inaccurately, so that the quality and the quantity of their learning is seriously impoverished. If we calculate how many hours some of our young learners spend actually 'doing' mathematics we might be surprised that they learn anything at all!

Inspection of these children's work books can sometimes show that they have had perhaps three or four sessions of work on a given topic. They have successfully completed only a few of the easier items each day and made many errors. On this scant evidence of mastery they move on, having 'done' that week's concept or procedure, to the next topic.

Children with difficulties in mathematics may resort to learning a few neat routines, such as 'doing sums', that have little or nothing to do with development of real mathematical thinking.

Action plans for successful learning

- Provide new learning experiences that will build on existing mathematical skills and understanding. Then already developed brain structures can be used as a starting point for new learning.
- Never move on to a new topic or increased level of difficulty before the pupil has mastered the easier levels of the task.
- Use graduated prompting to help the pupil acquire new understanding and skills.
- Use directed questioning to probe the pupil's understanding and to stimulate the development of the connections that are needed for successful learning.
- Provide explicit instruction in strategy and give guided practice (they practice, you guide).
- Ensure that mathematical learning experiences are introduced in stages. This allows the brain to acclimatise to new demands.
- Set up activities that the pupil can do with a little help, and then provide that help to promote real growth in the child's understanding.
- Recognise individual differences in the way in which your pupils can process different types of information and perform different tasks.
- Accept that pupils with dyscalculia may have extreme difficulty with some types of thinking (such as mental calculation) and offer alternatives (for example, a calculator).
- Provide enough time for practice and consolidation at each stage. This gives the brain time to get its wiring established and operating correctly before moving on to a more advanced or different topic.
- Revisit previously mastered skills often. This makes sure that the neurological circuits that underpin the skills keep in good shape.
- Work towards developing pupils' genuine understanding of mathematical concepts and procedures.
- Avoid teaching meaningless mechanical skills without developing understanding.
- Ensure that you use both verbal and non-verbal learning activities in your teaching.
- Modify how you teach to reflect the relative strengths and weaknesses that an individual pupil may have in the way in which they process information.

Chapter 3

MAKING MATHEMATICAL CONNECTIONS

Learning occurs in every moment of a child's life: in the kitchen, on the bus, visiting Grandma, having a shower, walking the dog, and even when they are at school!

Gersten (1999) points out that general mathematical thinking may be akin to phonological awareness in literacy: just as being attuned to markers in the language world give us clues about how spoken and written language 'works', so the general development of 'number sense' is an important prerequisite for later, more formal learning in mathematics.

Young children learn a vast amount of knowledge and understanding well before school they start school.

Did you know?

- 2-month-old babies can tell the difference between French and English.
- 5-month-old babies can count up to three.
- 5-month-old babies notice if a display is changed from two to three items.

(Mehler and Christophe, 1995; Canfield and Smith, 1996; Starkey and Gelman, 1990)

SEEING THE WORLD THROUGH MATHEMATICAL EYES

Some pupils will spontaneously think mathematically and see the world through mathematical eyes

Look at this conversation between 5-year-old Millie and an adult:

Adult: Hello Millie, come and sit here by me.

Millie: You've got eight books on your desk.

Adult: So I have!

Millie: Yes, three blue, three red, and two white ones.

> *Adult:* That's right, eight altogether.
>
> *Millie:* But you've really got ten because there are two missing. *(She is looking at the gaps in the array of books.)*
>
> *Adult:* Yes, I've got lots of books.
>
> *Millie:* That's not lots of books, ten books isn't lots of books. Lots of books is hundreds and hundreds of books like in the library.

Millie is a mathematical thinker, when she looks around her she sees mathematical patterns, in the same way as another child might notice people, colours or animals.

One of the most striking differences between children with dyscalculia and those who have good or exceptional capabilities in mathematics is that the children with mathematical difficulties do not seem to 'see' the mathematical world that they live in. They are not curious about mathematically related patterns and they probably engage in very little spontaneous mathematical thinking.

Have you ever had the experience of being on a tour where the guide makes you 'see' things that you would never have noticed by yourself? One of the skills of a good teacher is helping pupils recognise, and even become curious, about facets of their surroundings with which they have not spontaneously connected.

Being aware of the mathematical world which surrounds us is of critical importance in developing a sense of number. Many pupils with difficulties in learning mathematics probably only 'connect' with mathematical information when they are in situations that are explicitly called 'maths lessons'. This means of course that their learning environment is significantly impoverished, because they are only thinking mathematically for brief (and not necessarily successful) periods of time.

One of the most important foundations for confident learning in mathematics is to feel 'at home' in a mathematical world. If you do not even realise that you are living in a mathematical world, then of course it is very difficult for you to feel 'at home'.

Therefore before we try to address the specific, procedural difficulties that pupils with dyscalculia often experience, we must place a priority on setting them up so that they 'connect' with their mathematical surroundings outside of the lesson time when they officially 'do mathematics'.

MAKING CONNECTION WITH WHAT THE CHILD ALREADY KNOWS

Young children already know a lot before they start school. The trouble is that often that knowledge is not in the same sort of 'package' as they need at school. They may already play tea parties with their soft toys and always get out the right number of cups and saucers, and yet in school they may feel uncertain when they are asked to match the pictures that have 'the same' number of items.

Using real-life experiences that are already familiar to the children helps them to connect with what is being taught.

Sometimes children even have to unlearn things when they get to school! The 4-year-old who 'knows' the six on the dice just by looking may have to learn to touch count the same pattern when she gets to school.

> *Sue Willis (1990) tells this delightful anecdote:*
>
> *While playing a game with a 7-year-old, she started to write down the scores and add them up. The boy corrected her. The right way to do it was with 'running totals', adding numbers such as 27 and 54 onto the existing totals. He competently added the scores until they reached between 500 and 600.*
>
> *Later Sue noticed that in his school book he had been doing pages and pages of tens and units addition, but had always made errors in carrying from the units to the tens column.*
>
> *When she pointed this out to him and reminded him that he had been able to do these very same calculations mentally when they were playing their game he said,* No, they are not running totals, they are add ups and this is the way you do it. Our teacher told me that this is the way you do it.

LEARNING HAS TO MAKE SENSE AND FIT INTO THE BIG PICTURE

When children begin to learn mathematics it is all too easy for them to believe that mathematics is something you do only in school, perhaps after reading and before lunch.

Children may think that mathematics is just about learning a collection of facts, which has no overall pattern, logic or use. If so then they are missing the point of mathematics. Mathematics is all about patterns, connections and applications.

Unless they are shown the connections they may not realise that adding up is not just something that you do on a worksheet on Monday mornings, it is also something that happens when you work out how many people are coming to your birthday party, or how many eggs you have to get out of the fridge for breakfast.

Children with dyscalculia often find abstract calculation very difficult. If they can understand the link between real life and seemingly abstract procedures, it can make all the difference to the way in which they learn. Both visual imagery and language are important parts of internal mathematical thinking. Connecting with real objects and events helps to trigger a visual image and/or language that really does make sense.

> *When I was a kid and started school I found it really difficult to catch on to all those numbers and what you had to do with them: add up, take away, it didn't make any sense to me. Then one day my dad started to get me to think about it using our cows (we had a dairy farm). Suddenly it was all as clear as day. I could 'see' three cows and then two more coming into the dairy and then it was all so obvious – and very interesting to me!*
>
> *John, 32*

LEARNING IS BETTER IF IT OCCURS IN MULTIPLE CONTEXTS

If learning only occurs in one context then often the understanding is tied down to that single situation. We have probably all known the child who can 'do' subtraction on a subtraction worksheet, but cannot do the same calculation when they are given a worksheet with mixed addition and subtraction, or use subtraction to solve a word problem.

If you only learn about liquid measures by using the classroom measuring beakers, then you may not make the connection between what you have learned and how to choose the best buy from the soft drinks stall at the football.

The strongest sort of learning occurs when experiences from a wide range of situations are all pulled together to illustrate the concept that is being taught.

MAKING SENSE OF MANIPULATIVES

As teachers we'd probably all agree that real, hands-on learning is a far more powerful way of learning than dry, abstract instruction, especially for young children who are still at a 'concrete' stage of learning.

Quite rightly, we acknowledge that young pupils need to touch and have 'real' objects to work with as they begin to master the early formalities of mathematics. So we give them plastic counters, wooden blocks and special mathematics equipment in the hope that these items will be meaningful substitutes for the genuine, 'real' objects (such as toys, pets, apples, brothers, bikes, butterflies, cars or whatever else has absorbed the child's interest that day).

But for many young learners these 'manipulatives' may be just as mysterious as the written symbols that go with them. The pupils may learn to 'manipulate the manipulatives' but not transfer this to any understanding of what this manipulation actually represents. They may be able to look at a written algorithm and work out the answer with their Cuisenaire rods, and yet never make any connection with the broader concept as it applies in the real world.

> I never did really get what those little wooden blocks were all about. I said they were 'tens' and 'ones' because that's what the teacher said we had to call them, but it never, ever dawned on me that they could stand for anything real like ten kids, or ten dollars. They were just little bits of wood that we did things with. In the end I could do stuff with the blocks OK, but I can't say it ever really made any sense to me. It was only when I started teacher training and came across those same little wooden blocks again that I realised what it had all been about!
>
> *Rod, 39*

> *Some 6-year-olds were playing a game with a quite a difficult scoring system. Although the game itself was going well, the children were getting muddled (and argumentative!) about keeping the score accurately. As a visitor to their school I asked,* Why don't you use your counters? That would make it easy to keep the score.
>
> Oh no! They are for doing sums Miss, we don't use them when we're just playing.

Sometimes children learn to use one type of manipulative but fail to realise that the counters (or whatever they are using) are only being used as symbols or representatives of abstract numbers. Matthew (below) seems to think that addition is only something that happens with counters, and that the counters are therefore an intrinsic part of the process.

Adult: *What is 6 + 8?*

Matthew: *Can I have some counters? I can do it with counters.*

Adult: *Sorry, I haven't got any counters. Here, use these pencils instead.*

Matthew: *I don't know how to do it with pencils.*

GENERALISING LEARNING

What we teach in school is usually intended to be of some use or value in other situations beyond the mathematics lesson at school.

Children need to see how what they are learning connects with other learning and with life in general. They need to be able to apply the learning in new situations. They need to understand where it will, and where it will not be useful. And sometimes they need to be able to adapt the process as necessary.

We know that one of the major differences between a novice and an expert is that the experts can see the 'big picture'. They know the facts, but more importantly they understand how these facts relate both to each other, and to other, seemingly quite different, sets of knowledge. Interestingly they can then learn more facts very easily, because they can see how it all fits together.

PARENTS ARE IMPORTANT TEACHERS: HELP THEM TO MAKE THE CONNECTIONS

It is not surprising that children frequently see mathematics as the Monday worksheet. Often that is what their parents think too! Have you noticed how often when parents try to help their child with mathematics they give them worksheets in addition, subtraction, multiplication and division?

Adults draw on their own early experiences and remember that mathematics was learning multiplication tables, doing long division, or learning about fractions.

Often they translate this into what they teach their children at home, and what they expect the teacher to teach at school.

The experiences and learning that goes on at home and in the community can be very important elements in helping children to develop skills and confidence in mathematics.

UNDERSTANDING THE PURPOSE OF MATHEMATICS

Children with mathematical learning difficulties are often so bound up in the small, day-by-day struggles that they do not see the big picture of what mathematics is all about. If teaching emphasises the process rather than the purpose, then once again the children may fail to understand that mathematics is a real life skill.

We do math bacos we got to

We do maths so if we get to be a techer when we groow up we can do workshets for the kids in ower class

It is good to do math so your teacher won't get mad at you

Without seeing the purpose of mathematics the pupils will find it a lot more difficult to believe that the mathematics that they are learning is ever going to have any value or significance for them as individuals.

Action plans for succesful learning

- Make explicit connections between what you teach and the children's everyday lives. Always introduce a new skill or topic by linking it to the children's own experiences and lives.
- Look at how the children play and use mathematics in their everyday lives and build on that in the classroom. Make real-life experiences the beginning and the end points of the mathematics that you teach.
- Take the mathematics that you teach in the classroom out to into the playground, the environment, the sports field and the home.
- Emphasise *choosing* and *using* as vital mathematics skills. Children do not only need to know how to 'do' mathematics, they must be able to know which mathematical process to choose in a given situation and how to apply it in real life. *What sort of maths should we choose to work out the teams for sports day? What is the best way to find out how much paper we need for our display table? How can we work it out? Why couldn't we use times tables for this one?*
- Model estimation and approximation as important mathematical thinking skills in real life mathematics. Teach the pupils to make a distinction between when approximation and exact mathematics is needed. *Could we guess the number of tickets we need on the train? Could we estimate what time we have to leave for the swimming gala?*
- End each day with a recap of what the children have learned in their formal lessons. Have a 'Maths Wrap Up' every afternoon to highlight what they have learned or used informally: *We added up today when we worked out how many tickets we needed from the office. We measured today when we put the books on the shelf. We used fractions today when we shared our paints with Mr Jolley's class.*
- Always teach a new concept or skill in multiple contexts, across the curriculum. Find ways to link learning in other subjects with your mathematics curriculum.
- Always make the mathematical connections between what you are teaching and other learning explicit: *You remember that we were doing doubles and halves in maths the other day. Look in this book: it says that the pygmy mouse is half the size of the regular house mouse. So if a house mouse is 5 cm long, how long do you think a pygmy mouse would be?*

- Encourage all of your pupils to look for mathematical patterns and talk mathematical talk as part of their everyday life. For example:

A new pet rabbit
How much does the rabbit weigh?
How many babies do rabbits usually have in a litter?
How many rabbits could you get in a year if all the female babies had babies?
How much does the rabbit eat?
How long will one bag of rabbit food last?
How big is its hutch? Can you draw a plan of it?
How often does it have to be cleaned out?

A trip to visit grandma
How many days were you there for?
How long did the trip take?
How far did you have to travel? Can you draw a map of the trip?
How old is grandma?
What year was she born in?
How old was grandma when you were born?
Is she the oldest person you know?
Let's make a number line with your age and grandma's age.

- Use the calendar:
Make use of the calendar very explicit.
Have a large yearly planner on the wall, and mark off the days as they pass.
Mark in birthdays, special events etc.
Count down to exciting events such as sports day.
Have the pupils date all their work.
Talk often about the date and the season to help pupils get a sense of where they are in the year's cycle.

- Use reading, poetry, drawing and the children's own language:
Draw a map of where the story happened.
Draw a timeline for a Harry Potter story.
Make a scale model of the giant in the story.
Draw a family tree of the characters in the book.
Tell a mathematical story.

2 cars racing spiding at 299 per har number 6 is in frunt. the plane is olso going 299 as wel. the plane is going to Perth. Perth is 100 clomiters. there is 21 pepal on the plane. There is 20 pasingersa 1 pilct.

'2 cars racing, speeding at 299 per hour. Number 6 is in front. The plane is also going 299 as well. The plane is going to Perth. Perth is 100 kilometres. There is 21 people on the plane. There is 20 passengers and 1 pilot.'

- Make sure pupils understand that manipulatives represent real objects and can be used in a variety of ways to stand in place of items that are too large or inconvenient to use. Talk to the children explicitly about how manipulatives can be used as 'pretend' pigs, cars, boats, people etc.
- Run sessions so that parents can understand that their child's progress in mathematics depends not only on them being able to 'do sums', but much more importantly on their child feeling 'at home' in a mathematical world. You can photocopy the handouts at the end of this book: these have plenty of good ideas for parents.
- Play mathematical 'I spy':

I spy with my little eye something that is more than one metre long.
I spy with my little eye something that weighs less than 500 grams.
I spy with my little eye a triangle.
I spy with my little eye something that comes in thousands at a time.

- Class database: Make a class database on a computer spreadsheet. Have the pupils' ages, heights, favourite sports, personal best scores, pets, shoe sizes or anything else that is of interest. Update it regularly and give everyone a print-out. Use the spreadsheet graphics to put the information into several different formats. Give all pupils a turn to manage the data entry and the presentation on the spreadsheet.
- Let the children hear you using mathematics as you think aloud, for example counting off children as they leave the room, working out materials that are needed for an art lesson etc.

Chapter 4

ASSESSMENT

WHAT IS VALUED?

The clearest message about what is valued in the classroom is to look at what is recorded, assessed and reported on. Does the teacher record interesting but unsuccessful attempts at a difficult task, or does she only assess whether you get easy things right or wrong? Does she want to know how you thought things out, or does she want to see the right answer?

Does your teacher seem more pleased with a worksheet where you have plugged in the right answers or a difficult construction task which you nearly got right?

WHAT DOES COMPETENCE LOOK LIKE?

Many pupils have only a very shallow understanding of what mathematics competence looks like.

Saul and Petra had been trying to work out how they were going to raise funds at the school fete. They had talked, scribbled, calculated, written things down, discussed and worked away at the task. As two pupils with dyscalculia, they had used a range of tally marks, patterns, sketches and numbers in their attempts to work out their plan. As an adult approached them Saul rapidly screwed up their working notes and threw them in the bin.

What was that you just threw away Saul?

That was only rubbish, *said Saul.* It was really messy, *added Petra*

Having a work book full of ticks may look like mathematics competence. Having a sheet of paper full of false starts, tally marks and corrections may look like incompetence. Yet the latter may well be a much better example of good mathematical thinking.

In Chapter 1 we discussed how pupils with dyscalculia may have very variable performance in mathematics. A child may be gifted with spatial mathematics and yet have severe difficulties with simple arithmetic. Unfortunately the easiest areas of mathematics to assess are concrete calculation, recall of number facts and accurate implementation of mechanical working methods – the very areas that children with dyscalculia will find the most challenging to perform well in!

WORKING IT OUT YOUR OWN WAY

It is remarkable how seldom adults use the 'proper' way to work out a calculation. Even adults who do know the standard working methods in mathematics often use their own, quite idiosyncratic ways of working out an answer to an everyday life skills math problem. Adults quite often use very concrete ways of calculating, for example using fingers to work out how many days until a special date, and may use quite different working methods for the same problem at different times. Most often adults will rely on approximation rather than exact computation.

Many pupils with dyscalculia will need to be able to use their own idiosyncratic ways of working things out. They may find basic mental arithmetic difficult or have trouble remembering their tables. They may need aids such as a number square or a calculator; they may even devise their own ingenious ways of getting to the right answer.

David had trouble learning his tables. He had worked out that he only needed to know his odd times tables because then he could always work out answers to the even tables by addition (he was much better at mental addition than tables!).

If $4 \times 3 = 12$ then $4 \times 4 = 12 + 4 = 16$

If $5 \times 7 = 35$ then $5 \times 8 = 35 + 5 = 40$

If $6 \times 5 = 30$ then $6 \times 6 = 30 + 6 = 36$

If $8 \times 3 = 24$ then $8 \times 4 = 24 + 8 = 32$

For most of us this is much harder than learning all of the tables, and for many pupils with dyscalculia David's method would be really confusing. But for David it worked! Except that in mental arithmetic tests he always got the even number multiplication items wrong because his method took too long!

If you were his teacher would you say he was competent with all of his tables or not?

LET THE ERRORS TELL THE STORY

You will remember that earlier in this book we looked at how the best learning occurs at the boundaries of competence. Learning does not occur once competence has been achieved, or when competence is too far off.

If the children are making too many errors then you know that you have set the level of difficulty too far away from their boundary, and you need to adjust the tasks to an easier level.

If the children are getting everything correct then you know that the tasks are well inside their boundary of competence and that you need to extend your expectations of what they can do.

As teachers we need to watch for the errors that our pupils make. These mark out the boundary of their competence, and in turn that tells us where to direct our teaching.

But before we start to teach we have some detective work to do. Is there a pattern in the errors? Does the pupil always make the same mistake? Is there something that the pupil obviously does not understand? Does the pupil always leave something out? Is the pupil just plugging in numbers in an apparently random way?

One of the most valuable techniques we can use when working with pupils with dyscalculia is to ask them to think out loud so that we can track where their thinking is going.

> I just said 5 add 6 and then, and then 7. So I put 7 down there.
>
> How did you know it was 7?
>
> Because 7 comes after 6, and I said 6 and then I said 7, yes that's right, 5 add 6 is 7.

> $$\begin{array}{r} 26 \\ -18 \\ \hline 12 \end{array}$$
>
> Well I said to myself, 6 take away 8 you can't do, so pretend it's 8 take away 6, that's easy, that's 2.
>
> *By listening to Sam's internal monologue Sam's teacher discovered he did know 6 take away 8 you can't do rule, he just had his own method of dealing with it!*

Earlier we looked at using graduated prompting as a teaching technique for pupils with dyscalculia and other learning difficulties. Graduated prompting also has the potential to be a very sensitive and informative assessment tool.

As we prompt we can observe just how much help the child needs to be successful. Does the pupil just need us to redirect her attention to a salient feature of the problem (*Don't forget to look at the sign, Zoe*) or does she need more explicit direction (*Find the biggest number first and start from there*)? How does the pupil make sense of our prompts? Can she find the biggest number? Does she understand the sign and make appropriate use of it? Does she remember to look at the sign by herself without any prompts on the next item? How quickly can we fade the prompts out? Where are the sticking points?

DON'T GET CAUGHT NOT KNOWING

It's a strange fact that children who go to school to learn often believe that it is a bad thing to be caught not knowing something!

Often children will leave a blank in an answer rather than have a try and risk being wrong. Or say *I can't remember* when what they mean is *I don't know!* or *I don't understand.*

PUPILS WHO EVALUATE THEIR OWN LEARNING KNOW WHAT COUNTS

Some pupils wait passively for an adult to tell them whether what they have just done is good or bad. They have not engaged in thinking about their learning or attempted to evaluate it for themselves. They might not even know how to judge whether they were doing well or not.

> *Adult:* How are you getting along in math, Ashari?
>
> *Ashari:* I don't know. My teacher hasn't told me yet.

Knowing what you know and what you do not know is a very important part of taking responsibility for your own learning.

One really useful technique is to get pupils to check their own work: not just to mark it right or wrong depending on what answers the teacher calls out, but to review and evaluate what they have done.

They can check through and mark off those items where they are 100% confident that they are correct. They can use alternative methods to double check their answers, or consult with a classmate or adult on items where they are not certain. They can rework items they have got wrong and see if they can get them right. They can make notes to the teacher to comment on how they think they handled the tasks.

Action plans for successful learning

- Remember that what you assess tells your pupils what you value.
- Pupils with dyscalculia may excel in one area of mathematics and have difficulties in another, so always make sure that any mathematics assessment is segmented so that you and the pupil can see the pattern of successes and failures.
- Teach the children that competence is not just a page of ticks: it is thinking, reasoning, problem solving and sometimes getting the answer right! Give credit for thinking mathematically.
- Allow pupils with dyscalculia to use their own strategies if this works for them.
- Get the pupils to review their own work and to reconsider and consult where uncertainties exist.
- Make sure the children understand that 'not knowing' is an inevitable part of learning.
- Teach the pupils that 'not knowing' and then doing something about it is good learning.
- Ask the children to think out loud so you can learn to understand how they are thinking things through.
- Use graduated prompting as both a teaching and an assessment strategy.
- Use the children's errors as an important source of information.
- Get to know your pupils' boundaries of competence.

Chapter 5

INDIVIDUAL DIFFERENCES AND MATHEMATICS

There was once a school for animals. To make life easy for the teachers the headmaster decided to have the same curriculum and teaching method for everyone. All the animals had to do the same lessons and reach the same standards. The duck did extremely well in swimming, but found the singing lessons very difficult indeed. The rabbit was fine at the running and jumping lessons but became quite hysterical in the swimming lessons. The birds were top of the class for flying, but had to go to remedial tree-climbing.

At the end of the term the teachers met to see how their pupils had progressed. The rabbit had not come to school for weeks, his mother said he had a bad cold because of all that swimming, even though a teacher had seen him running and jumping in the fields. The duck was still a great swimmer but the teacher reported Very little progress. Could do better *in singing. The birds had been in detention three times, but they still flew to the top of the tree when they thought that the climbing teacher was not looking.*

Based on The Animal School *by George H. Reavis*

MATCHING TEACHING STYLE TO LEARNING STYLE

Some children are slow, reflective learners, while others like their learning to be fast-paced. Some use trial and error, others work systematically through the problem until they get to the end. Some rely on intuitive thinking, others prefer concrete, practical ways of working things out.

It is only effective to teach by talking if you have a pupil who learns by listening.

There is no one, 'right' learning style. The child who thinks slowly and reflectively may eventually produce a better solution than their impulsive classmate. But the trial-and-error learner may hit on the right solution almost immediately, or find several, equally good solutions to the same problem.

Pupils with dyscalculia will display a range of individual learning styles; confidence and motivation will add another dimension to the way in which they approach mathematics tasks.

Many children with learning difficulties will be impulsive and inattentive learners. Lacking understanding they may use trial and error, but fail to learn from their mistakes and repeat the same mistake over and over again.

Other pupils may be very dependent on slow, methodical, concrete working. They may carefully add totals such as *35 + 16* by counting in ones because they lack the skills or confidence to work it out by vertical addition.

Slow workers will miss out on essential practice if they only work for the same amount of time as other pupils.

> *Here is a little mathematics problem for you to work out yourself:*
>
> Jack only completes 6 out of the 10 items on his work sheet today.
>
> The other pupils complete all 10 items.
>
> If he always works at the same rate, what percentage of practice will he have missed by the end of the school year?
>
> If there are 40 weeks in the school year, what is the equivalent number of weeks of schooling in mathematics that Jack will have missed by working slowly?
>
> *Answers: Jack will have missed 40% of the available practice.*
> *Jack will have missed the equivalent of 16 weeks of schooling in mathematics.*

USING THE THEORY OF MULTIPLE INTELLIGENCES

We all know that different children learn in different ways. What fascinates one child will have little or no appeal to another. What one child finds easy, another will find difficult. Every pupil with dyscalculia will also have an array of preferred learning styles and their own unique profile of intelligence. What does the theory of multiple intelligences tell us about how children with dyscalculia might be expected to deal with mathematical learning?

VERBAL-LINGUISTIC INTELLIGENCE

These children love to talk, to read and to write. They like to learn new words, and they enjoy experimenting with their language. They will often ask what words mean and enjoy verbal jokes such as puns and riddles. If you talk, they will usually listen. They will often learn best by talking their way through a task.

Mathematics that is presented as diagrams, shapes or numbers on a sheet may seem like unknown territory to these pupils.

Mathematics that uses words, and relates to language-rich areas will be much more appealing. The pupil who cannot 'see' a mathematical pattern in numbers or shapes may instantly recognise the rhyming pattern of a poem.

Some of these pupils may have dyscalculia: their verbal brightness may be in sharp contrast to their difficulties with mathematical calculation or visuospatial reasoning. Their mathematical difficulties will be most evident when they are dealing with abstract mathematical concepts that are difficult to verbalise.

INTERPERSONAL INTELLIGENCE

These children place a priority on person-to-person relationships and communication with others. In school they like learning collaboratively, and they may find solo work difficult to enjoy.

These pupils love socialising, and their play activities nearly always involve others.

They are socially aware, and are very often caring and concerned for others. They see things from other people's perspectives as well as their own.

If mathematics connects with real people and real social issues they will often be your keenest pupils.

Social approval will also be very important to this group of pupils, and this may have an impact on the way they approach mathematics. If they have dyscalculia they may fear disapproval or social embarrassment. They may become very anxious, and try to avoid doing mathematics or to disguise or deny their difficulties.

If mathematics deals with inanimate objects, abstract patterns or problems that do not have a 'human interest' factor, then these pupils will find little to interest them.

Knowing *12 × 7 = 84* might not make a connection with anything that matters to them. Finding out that 12 homeless people go to the soup kitchen for a hot meal every day of the week may make the figures come to life in a way that makes them vitally important.

> *Your teaching may fall victim to the* Who cares? *factor if it does not connect with real human issues.*

KINESTHETIC INTELLIGENCE

These children's recreations will probably include sports, athletics, or informal physical activities such as climbing, swimming and running. They may enjoy gymnastics and pushing their body to its physical limits. Movement and tactile sensation are often very important and dynamic elements in their learning.

They learn best when they can move, and have physical action involved in their activity.

Mathematics that allows them to handle real objects, move around and remain physically active will hold their interest much more effectively than extended periods of desk work.

Mathematics that connects with physical activity such as sport will often be very engaging.

NATURALIST INTELLIGENCE

These children are interested and concerned about the environment. Often they are very observant about what is going on around them in terms of the changing seasons of the year, weather patterns and natural cycles of life.

Children with a high degree of naturalist intelligence are usually interested and concerned in big world issues such as global warming, conservation and recycling. They are often very knowledgeable about the natural world, and have a considerable knowledge base on topics of interest such as reptiles or marine animals.

These pupils may find that the mathematics that they are taught makes little connection with what matters to them. The *Who cares?* factor will often be significant.

> *7-year-old Dan was having difficulty with the new mathematics they were doing in class. He stubbornly refused to use any of the available manipulatives, despite requests to do so.*
>
> *Eventually he told us why:* None of those things are biodegradable you know ... I don't like touching them ... I think about how they will still be here in hundreds of years time ... I don't like them.
>
> *Although we might say that Dan's response was impractical, his emotional concerns for the environment dominated his response and blocked his ability to get on with the task.*

MUSICAL, RHYTHMIC INTELLIGENCE

These children understand rhythm, pitch and tune, and are natural 'performers' in music and possibly dance.

Such pupils are very sensitive to sounds, and responsive to the mood of music. Children with high musical intelligence often interpret music, and create meaning from what they hear. Often they are very aware of rhythmic patterns and can 'hold' a complex tune or rhythm with accuracy.

Music and rhythm have a natural affinity with mathematics and it may be that these musically talented pupils are also blessed with good mathematical potential.

They will tend to find it easy to recognise auditory patterns and shapes. For instance, they may 'hear' the pattern *in 37, 47, 57, 67, 77, 87* and be able to follow on with what 'sounds' right without any obvious mathematical calculation.

These pupils may work best in a very quiet environment if they are especially sensitive and responsive to sounds.

INTRA-PERSONAL INTELLIGENCE

These children are very aware of their own internal feelings and thought processes. They can often be single-minded, and 'march to the beat of their own drum'. They may prefer working alone and may be independently strong-willed. They like to learn things their way and are most interested in things that relate to themselves.

In mathematics these pupils may vary in their application. One day they are preoccupied with their own internal thinking, the next day they connect with the mathematics that is going on in the classroom around them.

If these children have difficulties with mathematics they may simply 'switch off' and take no further interest in the subject.

> *Your teaching may fall victim to the* It's nothing to do with me *factor if it does not connect with the child's own personal interests.*

If a mathematics topic does connect with this pupil's own personal interest then you may see a dramatic surge in interest while that topic is being taught. Warning! These interests tend to come and go in bursts of enthusiasm: what works once may not work again at a later stage.

> *Carol had really become involved when the mathematics she was doing related to her horse. Two months later her teacher tried to revive the interest, to no avail.*
>
> *Teacher:* But Carol, you loved doing this last term.
>
> *Carol:* Yes, but that was when I was really into horses.
>
> *Teacher:* So, you've gone off horses now?
>
> *Carol:* Oh yes. They're really boring. Now I'm into skating.

SPATIAL INTELLIGENCE

These pupils like to work with patterns, puzzles, mazes, graphics and designs. They may be very skilled at drawing and construction. They like visual information such as pictures, photographs, videos and slides.

They are often able to manipulate what they 'see' and so find it easy to deal with symmetry and mathematical problems that involve working with patterns and designs.

The spatial aptitudes of these pupils will give them real strengths in some areas of mathematics, where they need to use visual reasoning and problem solving.

These pupils may be paradoxical mathematics pupils, having outstanding capabilities with some high order mathematics skills and yet significant difficulties with what are usually seen as the 'simple' basics, such as mental arithmetic or basic word problems. They may need to turn word problems into visual images in their heads before they can work out the right way to deal with the question.

Ben is now a talented artist and designer, who recalled ongoing battles with teachers who always wanted him to show his working when he completed the mathematical elements for any design plans:

The trouble was I never did any working out. I don't do any now either, I think numbers and I know the answer. It's weird, but it's like asking me to 'Show your working for saying that this is a red chair', I can't tell you how I know, I just do. It seems so obvious to me.

Ben is probably accessing the mathematical information he needs through a whole-picture thinking process that is, for him, automatic. The patterns of numbers make so much sense to him so that he can 'see' totals just by looking at them in his mind's eye. If he has to break those patterns down into small segments to 'do' arithmetic he loses the clear picture that he had to begin with. As a child he was in a special mathematics class because he could never show his working or remember how to do calculations 'properly'. He became bored and disruptive and was thought to have a specific mathematics difficulty.

LOGICAL-MATHEMATICAL INTELLIGENCE

Children with high logical-mathematical intelligence see mathematical patterns and enjoy thinking about numbers. They look for patterns and logical sequences in things and may enjoy playing in a methodical way. They may enjoy collecting things, and keeping them in a systematic order.

Mathematics and science are often their favourite subjects.

Children with high logical-mathematical intelligence are probably the only group of pupils who will enjoy doing mathematics for its own sake. Although they may be interested in applied mathematics they may be equally absorbed in abstract mathematics that has no obvious external use or application.

Pupils with high logical-mathematical intelligence will readily become frustrated with hands-on learning in situations where they can already work at a highly abstract level. They too may have trouble showing their working because a lot of mathematical information is automatically recalled when needed.

AESTHETIC INTELLIGENCE

These pupils are very aware of their sensory surroundings. They gravitate towards things which have physical harmony or beauty, and love colours, textures and perfumes. They may be unsettled or repelled by things that are ugly and unpleasant.

Although they may delight in designs, they may not 'connect' with the mathematical regularity in these patterns. They will only see what is pleasing to the eye.

The physical presentation of mathematics may have a big impact, one way or the other. The colours and textures of manipulatives may make a mathematics activity very appealing. A dull, poorly photocopied worksheet may have the opposite effect.

Action plans for successful learning

- Identify the different learning styles of your pupils.
- Explicitly identify the type of thinking that is needed for a particular task: *For this you will need to think very, very carefully, Now you need to go fast on this one see how many you can do in a minute, just guess the ones you don't know.*
- Give time for the slow, reflective worker to complete the necessary work.
- Recognise that what appeals to one child may have exactly the opposite effect on another. Provide a range of alternative ways of dealing with the same topic.
- Create worksheets and activities that are theme-related. The content can be the basic mathematics curriculum. The focus can be the environment, literature, art, music, sport or human interest.
- Try self-directed activities: *Today we are going to work on our four times tables. You can write a story, you can draw a picture, you can build with blocks, write a song, make a pattern, invent a game or write a real or imaginary report. Whatever you do, you have to use at least part of the four times table. We'll talk about all your different ideas when you have all finished.*

Chapter 6
CONFIDENCE AND MATHEMATICS

EFFECTIVE LEARNING ENVIRONMENTS FOSTER SELF-CONFIDENCE

All policy makers and practitioners agree that confidence is a critical ingredient in successful learning. For example, the National Curriculum states that teachers need to create effective learning environments in which

- the contribution of all pupils is valued
- all pupils can feel secure and are able to contribute appropriately
- stereotypical views are challenged and pupils learn to appreciate and view positively differences in others (whether arising from race, gender, ability or disability)
- the pace of work is planned and monitored so that the pupils all have a chance to learn effectively and achieve success
- action is taken to maintain interest and continuity of learning for pupils who may be absent for extended periods of time
- teachers use appropriate assessment approaches that allow for different learning styles and ensure that pupils are given a chance and encouragement to demonstrate their competence and attainment through appropriate, familiar means
- clear and unambiguous feedback is provided to pupils to aid further learning
- individuals are helped to manage their emotions and take part in learning through
- aspects of learning in which the pupil will engage are identified and short-term, easily achievable goals and selected activities are planned
- positive feedback is provided to reinforce and encourage learning and build self-esteem
- tasks and materials are selected sensitively to avoid unnecessary stress for the pupil
- a supportive learning environment is created in which the pupil feels safe and is able to engage with learning
- time is allowed for the pupil to engage with learning and gradually increasing the range of activities and demands.

For pupils with dyscalculia, one of the major deciding factors with regards to whether they succeed or fail will be their levels of confidence, and in turn this will depend on how well their teachers have implemented appropriate teaching methods.

CONFIDENCE GROWS FROM THE BELIEF THAT YOU CAN SUCCEED

Confidence only develops through performance and action. Pupils will never become confident at mathematics unless they actually do it and experience success. Confidence does not transfer easily from one area to another: if you are a great swimmer but poor at mathematics then your confidence is likely to be high in swimming and low in mathematics.

Confidence has a very strong link with motivation. Generally speaking, motivation comes from the reasonable hope of success. The more confident you are, the more you are able to hope for success and the more motivated you will be! Because confidence is so closely linked to personal performance, it can quite easily be destroyed by just one or two difficulties or failures.

One of the best ways of judging pupils' confidence in themselves is to look at their willingness to perform a task or skill. Confident pupils will swing into action and tackle tasks that they believe they can attempt successfully. Children with low self-confidence will often be low in motivation and application.

ANXIETY DISRUPTS THINKING

Mathematics requires thinking that is controlled, orderly and sustained. Unfortunately this type of thinking is particularly vulnerable to disruption by anxiety. Pupils with dyscalculia are at high risk of anxiety-related learning difficulties, and underlying weaknesses in mathematical reasoning will be significantly exaggerated if the child becomes anxious about failure.

Anxiety can be provoked by

- looking at work and believing that it is too difficult to begin;
- starting a task and finding that it is bewildering so that you do not know how to proceed;
- being anxious about asking for help, for fear that you will be told that you should have listened;
- being reluctant to ask for help in case you are told that you should be able to work it out for yourself;

- fear about consequences, such as failing a test;
- expectations that parents may be angry if you do not do well at school;
- expectations that other children may ridicule or put you down, if they see that you are performing poorly in mathematics.

Community attitudes to mathematics

While many people in the community do of course enjoy mathematics, and may well use it extensively in their school, university or workplace, there are others who are equally in awe of mathematics. This attitude may well filter down to the children, so they expect that mathematics is going to be difficult and confusing.

Action plans for successful learning

- When teaching it is important to make sure that pupils have enough opportunity to practice a skill. Many pupils (especially those who find learning hard) barely master one skill before they have to move on to the next. Just being able to scrape through a task, with very fragile understanding, does not build confidence. Being able to do a task or demonstrate a skill with ease because you have had sufficient practice establishes a solid base of confidence.
- As indicated by the National Curriculum, it may be appropriate to place pupils in groups or sets, according to mathematical ability, or to give them an individual programme.
- Ensure that the level of difficulty matches the child's 'boundary of competence'. Work that is too easy will give them the message that they are seen as poor mathematics pupils (*She must think I'm thick to give me stuff like this*). Being given work that is too difficult makes the pupil feel stressed, anxious and very uncomfortable.
- Allow children to select their own level of difficulty. Provide various levels of scaffolding and let them decide how hard they will make the task: *This looks hard ... I'll use the resource folder to get myself started and I will ask my buddy to help. This looks OK, I'll try it without the calculator.*
- Encourage pupils to set their own learning goals, monitor their own progress and celebrate their own success: *My goal is to learn to do this sort of multiplication by Friday. I will know that I can do it well when I can do 15 of them with no more than three errors.*

- Confidence is related to performance in a specific skill. It does not readily transfer across from one skill area to another. So ensure that the pupil has enough teaching and practice in mathematics to experience success.
- Encourage the pupils to map their own progress and competence. Provide a simplified chart showing the main learning goals that you have in mind for the pupil. Work with them to identify what has already been mastered and where they are heading next. Record progress as it occurs.
- Use appropriate teaching techniques such as guided practice (you guide, they practice) and graduated prompting (the teacher gives the pupil prompts. At first the prompts are very explicit and directive, gradually they are faded away as the child gains skills and confidence. At no time is the pupil left to fail.).
- Connect mathematics to the child's real, everyday world, so that they feel 'at home' with the mathematical concepts being taught.
- Recognise that the pupil may have difficulties in language skills, visuospatial skills, or memory, which may impede their progress in mathematics so that they need additional support.
- Parental influence will be important. Parents who place pressure on their child to perform to an unrealistically high standard will be counter-productive.
- Parent's anxiety often stems from lack of understanding. Communicate with your pupils' parents, so that they understand how mathematics is taught at school, and how they can contribute to their children's progress.
- Recognise that while pupils with dyscalculia may have significant difficulties in some areas in the mathematics curriculum, they may be able to do well in others. Provide appropriate support such as calculators, number squares, printed times tables etc, which can support the pupil in their specific area of mathematical difficulty.
- Encourage your pupils to be test checkers not test takers. When they have an assessment, encourage them to evaluate their own work, reviewing it, discussing it, and revisiting items where they had difficulties, to make appropriate corrections through discussion and subsequent understanding.
- Modify assessments to meet individual needs. For instance, a pupil with dyscalculia who has poor auditory short-term memory will run into difficulties with mental arithmetic tests, because they will not be quick enough at remembering questions to work out the answers. Provide the test in an alternative form such as one that pupils can do in their own time, or an individually administered test, where an adult reads the questions out as often and slowly as is required by the pupil.

- Recognise that for anxious pupils with mathematical difficulties, a very crowded work sheet can produce an instant panic reaction. Ensure that all materials are clearly set out, and well spaced. It is better to have two or three work sheets, with clearly set out work than one where a lot of work is pushed into a small space.
- Try to make mathematics fun, by introducing games, sports, and across the curriculum activities, which reinforce the mathematical concepts, skills and knowledge base that you are working on with your class.
- Recognise that all pupils need varying degrees of concrete support. Allow the pupil with dyscalculia to continue using concrete support for as long as necessary, without undue comment or discouragement.

UNDERSTANDING THE NUMBER SYSTEM

In order to be able to understand and apply mathematics, the pupil must first develop an adequate understanding of the number system itself. Mathematics knowledge and understanding is accumulative, and without a firm foundation all subsequent learning will be difficult and very poorly grounded. The following chapters deal with the establishment of the basic concepts of the number system.

Chapter 7

INTRODUCTION TO UNDERSTANDING THE NUMBER SYSTEM

DYSCALCULIA AND THE NUMBER SYSTEM

Children, adolescents and adults with dyscalculia generally lack an intuitive sense of the number system. As a result they

- rely very heavily on concrete counting and mechanical calculation;
- experience difficulty with estimation and approximation;
- fail to notice errors and inconsistencies in their own work;
- have difficulties in performing mental calculations accurately.

The double disadvantage: dyscalculia and poor foundation learning

The difficulties experienced by pupils with dyscalculia are often significantly exaggerated by poor foundation learning. While dyscalculia makes it more difficult for a child to acquire basic number skills, most can, eventually, acquire a reasonable degree of understanding if they are given the right opportunities.

One of the most easily remedied stumbling blocks for pupils with dyscalculia is their lack of sufficient early and ongoing experience in basic counting and recording. Often they have been moved on too quickly to operations that assume an underlying knowledge of the number system which they do not yet possess.

Many children with dyscalculia are disadvantaged by

- insufficient early experience of the number system
- insufficient instruction in the way the number system works
- insufficient time and opportunity to gain skills in using the number system
- being moved on to more abstract work before they understand the basics
- learning to 'muddle through' without understanding
- a defeatist and negative attitude towards mathematics.

As pupils in middle and upper primary school, these children may receive remedial intervention. Their teacher will have the unenviable job of trying to clear away the fog of several years of confusion on top of very inadequate foundations. Misperceptions may be firmly embedded and incorrect working habits strongly established. Added to this, the pupil often has a negative and defeatist attitude towards mathematics, and towards themselves as mathematicians! All of this will take a lot of time, effort and expertise to reverse.

Thorough teaching of the basics of number concepts in the early years is therefore a very wise investment. It is much easier to establish a sound understanding of the number system and then teach the more abstract concepts than it is to undo years of misunderstanding and frustration. Making sure that the pupil has reached the appropriate level of readiness for the next step in the curriculum is critically important.

> *Saul could 'do' tens and units addition but when regrouping was introduced he floundered.*
>
>   14
>   +12
>   ‾‾‾‾‾
>
> *Asked to explain how he was doing this sum he explained,* See it's two sums pushed together, it's 2 and 6, that's the answer.

In comparison to another pupil of similar age and intelligence the pupil with dyscalculia will need

- more intensive, explicit teaching about the number system
- much more practice in using the number system
- an extended period of time to acquire the basics
- concrete experience with both large and small numbers.

As you read this section you will be aware that many of the strategies suggested are the 'normal' strategies that you would probably use for any pupil learning mathematics. For the pupil with dyscalculia these strategies do work, but only when they are presented in a more deliberate and intensive way, over a longer period of time and revisited frequently.

Essential competencies needed to understand the number system include the skills to

- count accurately and apply the skill of counting flexibly;
- understand how to use the base 10 system in counting;
- understand place value in written numbers;
- understand the composition and decomposition of numbers;
- have a strong sense of the order of magnitude of numbers and their relationship with each other.

Without these fundamentals, understanding more abstract or complex mathematical concepts or processes will prove to be very difficult indeed.

Chapter 8

COUNTING

The ability to count is, of course, an absolute basic in mathematics.

However, the simple mechanical process of 'counting' by saying the numbers in sequence is only the first part of the process. Far more important is the development of an underlying understanding of how the system 'works'.

Many older children (and indeed some adults) may still have difficulties with some aspects of counting, such as 'counting on' in addition, or using patterns such as counting in multiples of 2, 5 or 10. They may also have continuing problems with the more abstract elements, such as understanding and using hundreds, thousands and millions.

Earlier in this book we talked about the importance of a pupil feeling 'at home' with numbers, and counting is really where it all begins. Let us look at some of the core skills needed to count accurately and flexibly.

SAYING THE CORRECT SEQUENCE

Some children with dyscalculia have particular difficulties in remembering sequences, even when they have heard them many times before. They may muddle the recitation of a nursery rhyme or the alphabet and have difficulties with remembering and reciting the sequence of numbers when they count. For example, they may count *1, 2, 3, 4 … 8, 9, 20,* or lack fluency as they count *1, 2, 3, 4 … 4 …. 4 … 5, that's right … 5 … 6 … um, 6 … 6 … 7, 8, 9, 10.*

Sometimes they may try to use a rule that they have learned to help them count.

Sally understands that when you count you add on single digits to the starting point of 20, so that you count twenty, twenty one, twenty two, twenty three, twenty four, twenty five, but she misapplies this rule by counting on twenty six, twenty seven, twenty eight, twenty nine, twenty ten, twenty eleven, twenty twelve.

USING 1:1 CORRESPONDENCE WHEN COUNTING

This kind of 1:1 correspondence means that the pupil can co-ordinate counting with touching or looking (touch the first item, say *one*, touch the next item, say *two*). It is hampered by counting difficulties. If the child is still uncertain in saying the sequence of numbers, then the distraction of touching the item may make the pupil lose track of where they were in the counting process.

Some pupils with dyscalculia can recite a sequence of numbers at great speed, producing a blur of words, *onetwothreefourfivesix ...,* but they lack the more subtle skills of true counting, in that they cannot easily use and apply this sequence in a meaningful way.

Even when they can count accurately, some pupils with dyscalculia may find the integration of two modalities (touching and speaking) difficult, even though they can do each in isolation quite easily.

Automaticity in counting in an essential beginning point for all later activities in mathematics. Automaticity means that not only can the child say the sequence of numbers, at first to ten and then beyond, but that they can manipulate the way they say it.

Action plans for successful learning

- If the child has serious difficulties with touch counting, start with an easier 'touch and talk' task. Have a row of coloured buttons where the child has to touch and name the colour, for example *red, blue, blue, red, yellow, blue, red*: this is an easier task than remembering a number sequence and co-ordinating touching and talking.
- Sufficient practice is essential to develop true automaticity. Remember that counting is an activity that becomes 'hard wired' in the brain and that practice is essential.
- Get the child to move, pick up or cross off the items as they count: this is slightly more tangible and less abstract than touching and counting.
- Develop skills in looking and counting (without actually touching), as this is one step towards visualisation and abstract counting. Place an array of items in front of the pupil and ask them to count them by looking, not touching. Children with dyscalculia often get stuck in a very concrete stage where they do not trust themselves to count without touching. For some it is truly difficult, for others they can do quite well if they are given the opportunity to try out the skill in a safe situation.

USING COUNTING SKILLS FLEXIBLY

Good counting skills include the ability to control the way in which a sequence of numbers is said, such as being able to

- vary the speed of counting to match a physical action (such as touching or lifting);
- stop at a desired point;
- continue on from a given point;
- count in reverse;
- decide what type of counting to use in a given situation (count in multiples of one, two, five, ten or one hundred) and use the chosen method effectively.

These counting skills are essential foundations for later mathematical learning. Pupils need to be able to stop at the right place when they are measuring or counting out a subset. They need to be able to 'count on' in addition and 'count back' in subtraction. They need to use the most efficient way of counting for a given situation.

Pupils with dyscalculia often find it difficult to abstract the concept of counting beyond ten, so that additional, specific counting experiences, using real objects in large quantities, is necessary to help them develop a solid understanding of the number system.

Many pupils with dyscalculia continue on with concrete counting for many years, and do not use cardinal numbers in their mathematical thinking (a cardinal number is the last one in a sequence, if you count five objects the cardinal number is 5). Mechanical counting (and recounting) is cumbersome and time-consuming and prevents the pupil from using more efficient means of calculation, such as 'counting on' in addition.

Action plans for successful learning

- Give the pupils extensive practice in counting across a wide range of situations. For pupils with dyscalculia, explicit teaching and practice is essential to take them through to larger numbers once the first, easy counting has been mastered.
- Do a real-life stocktake in the classroom, stationery cupboard or school sports cupboard, and get the pupils with mathematics difficulties to help you. Get them to make up their own record sheet to keep track of the counting, using tally marks or numbers. Encourage grouping of items into tens to aid easy counting and checking.

- Take every opportunity to count out loud in class and encourage children to count with you. Vary the rate at which you count, quick and fluent when you count out small items such as pencils, slow and uneven when you are counting groups of children around the room: *1, 2, 3 … 4, 5, 6, 7, 8 … 9, 10 … 11, 12 … 13, 14, 15, 16, 17, 18 … 19, 20.*
- Create opportunities to practise the skill of counting to a given number and then stopping (this is a lot harder than counting a set of items until they are all counted): *We need 12 pencils, take 12 pencils out of the box.*
- Model the process of 'counting on' from a predetermined number and encourage the children to join in *We have 8 chairs already, now lets see, we've got another 4 here, so that's 8 … 9, 10, 11, 12.* This will help to prepare children for the later skill of 'counting on', which they will need for addition.
- Model the process of counting in reverse and encourage the children to join in. Instead of counting in ascending order as the children leave the room, count backwards: *22, 21, 20, 19, 18, 17, 16, 15 …*
- Use games and activities that all involve counting, especially counting larger numbers such as keeping a cricket or basketball score.
- Have a wide range of things to count that will interest and delight the children. As well as specially designed mathematics equipment (such as counters, Dienes blocks, Cuisenaire rods, Unifix cubes etc) use real-life objects such as books; stickers; crayons; stationary items; toy cars; zoo, marine and farm animals; food, and attractive, tactile materials such as coloured ribbons; interesting buttons; beads or marbles; coloured papers; old greeting cards; sea shells; pebbles etc.
- Remember to reflect the children's diverse intelligences. Have counting activities that involve physical activities like running, skipping, jumping and throwing and catching, connect counting to families, neighbourhoods and real people, use interesting things from the environment and the visual and musical world.
- Encourage grouping by ten as the children count.
- Expose the pupils to as much number vocabulary as possible. Encourage the pupils to talk about their counting, using words such as *more, less, none, nearly as many, enough, just the same amount, fewer, extra, hardly any, only two, that is not enough, there are none left.* Being able to 'translate' counting information into everyday language is a crucial mathematical skill.
- Give explicit teaching so that pupils understand that the question *How many?* needs a cardinal number as an answer, for example 8, not the counting sequence *1, 2, 3, 4, 5, 6, 7, 8.*
- Get the children to help you check off a delivery of items against the order sheet or delivery note.

CLASSIFICATION AND COUNTING

Classification is usually an essential element of meaningful counting. We do not need to know that we have *6* or *5* but we do need to know that we have *six children waiting to use the computer* or *five children who have finished their reading assignment.* Linking counting with classification gives the process a meaning and relevance that helps the number system to 'come alive' for the child with dyscalculia.

Many pupils with dyscalculia get so bound up in the difficulties of mechanical counting that they lose sight of the fact that counting is meant to be a purposeful activity, linked to practical uses and applications.

To the child with dyscalculia, however, counting may seem to be an abstract process that you 'do' with abstract materials without understanding how or why. If this is so then it follows that any type of mathematical concept that relates to the number system will also be poorly understood. You may be able to count to ten and say that *5+5 = 10,* but not connect this to real life and practical applications.

Action plans for successful learning

- Use your environment to generate interesting and useful counting and classification activities. *How many trees in the park? How many species? How many types of birds do we see? How many of them? Which are the rarest?*
- Encourage parents to develop their children's counting skills. They might help to tidy the garage and sort out and count nuts, bolts, screws etc and put them into containers. They could sort their clothes as a tidying/counting activity: *How many T shirts do you have? How many socks does the baby have? Can you count them in pairs or one by one?*
- Encourage the children to collect, sort, count and talk about things that interest them. Give them the opportunity to work on their collections, cataloguing, counting, recording and discussing.
- Develop skills in classification and cross classification as part of counting. Even something as simple of a collection of stones and pebbles can be sorted according to various criteria: *6 grey, 2 white, 5 black, 7 brown ... most of the pebbles are brown, there are only 2 white ones, there are no red ones.*
- Put a selection of interesting counting items (craft materials, toy animals, buttons or beads, picture postcards, shells, leaves etc) into a mixed heap in the

---

middle of the table. You can use a single category (such as buttons) and get the children to make classifications within that set *metal buttons, blue buttons, red buttons etc.* Alternatively, you can provide a wonderful mixture of items that have to be sorted and counted – socks, buttons, paint brushes, pebbles, Christmas decorations – and let the children sort and count.

Get the children to sort the items into logical categories and then do 'packing' where they have to put items into containers (jars, boxes, paper bags etc) and then label the containers to show the number of items in each.

Encourage the use of groups of tens for sorting and counting.

Use a simple record sheet so that the pupils can record the number of items they are counting.

This task links into the use of written numbers, and also into volume and shape: *Will all the buttons fit in that little box? What shape box should we use for those long, thin sticks?*

- Take the opportunity to use mathematical language as you talk to the children about the classification and counting activity: *I think this box has the most animals in it… This jar has got fewer things in it … there are not many in here.*
- Show the pupils how to use a simple, pictorial computer spreadsheet to record their counting and classification.

COUNTING IN ANY ORDER, COUNTING EACH ITEM ONCE

Most children with mathematical difficulties do understand these two concepts quite readily. However, often they run into difficulties when they have to put the ideas into practice.

The pupil may just scatter manipulatives or tally marks which are being used to assist with arithmetic operations such as addition. The messy organisation makes it very difficult to follow the *count only once* rule. They may try to count their manipulatives in *any order* but in doing so get muddled and either double count or omit items.

Often the problem lies in the pupil's poor spatial skills, where they do not 'see' how to organise manipulatives or tally marks in a logical pattern and so try to work from a disorderly array of items.

Action plans for successful learning

- Encourage the pupil to arrange counting materials in a systematic way rather than randomly scattered, to assist with accurate counting.
- At a later stage, when manipulatives or tally marks are being used to support arithmetic, give explicit instruction and skills practice in using a system to organise counting materials in an orderly way. At this stage organising the materials or tally marks in tens is especially useful.

Chapter 9

UNDERSTANDING THE BASE 10 SYSTEM

BASE 10 AND DYSCALCULIA

In our number system there are repeated patterns which generally help to make the number system easy to use. We can count in tens, or fives, or twos (or any other number we like) and find a pattern in the sequence. However, the number ten and its multiples and factors has particular usefulness because, of course, it is the basic 'building block' of our number system.

We can add or subtract 10 or 100 or 1000 easily from any number, by using the pattern of the numbers that we hear and say. However, children with dyscalculia often do not understand the recurring patterns and so cannot make use of them when counting or trying to think mathematically. Whilst they can *say* the sequence *2, 4, 6, 8, 10*, or *20, 30, 40, 50, 60, 70* etc they may not necessarily use these skills in every day counting real objects.

A clear understanding of 10s, 100s,1000s and beyond is an essential foundation for understanding very large numbers.

> *Tom was 13 years old. He was given a carton of screws for a woodwork project. The screws were all in labeled packets of ten. Tom was asked to check that there were 500 screws in total, as this number was required for the class. He opened all the packets, tipped all the screws into a pile and then counted them one by one! He said there were 498.*
>
> *Like many pupils with dyscalculia, Tom relies on one-by-one counting, even though he can count in tens quite accurately when asked to do so. He often produces inaccurate answers when he tries to count large quantities, because he counts one by one and loses track of what he has counted and what he has not. Because of his poor number sense he did not realise that if all the packets had contained 10 screws then a total of 498 was bound to be incorrect.*

Mental computation is heavily dependent on having a good intuitive understanding of the number system and an ability to use patterns such as 2s, 5s,10s, 100s. Children with dyscalculia frequently have major deficits in these fundamentals and as a result have notable difficulties with mental computation.

Try this with a pupil who has difficulties with mathematics:

What is 5 + 10?
What is 17 + 10?
Take 10 away from 99.
Add 100 to 163.
Take 100 away from 105.
What is 17 + 9?

Do they try to count the answers or do they just 'know' without having to calculate?

Do you think that they understand the way the patterns of 10 and 100 work?

Are they treating these numbers like any others using a mechanical counting system to arrive at the answer?

Is it easier for them to work out 17 + 10 than it is to work out 17 + 9?

Do they go through the same thinking process for both of these questions?

Action plans for successful learning

- Use a number line to count in 10s and 100s and then 1000s so that the pupils have a visual representation of the number system.
- Observe your pupils' working methods when they are counting large quantities. If they are counting one by one, demonstrate how to group and count in tens, so that they see the practical usefulness of being able to use a quick alternative to counting in ones.
- Get the pupils to bring in items that are packed in 10s or 100s (hardware and stationary stores are particularly good sources of prepackaged items). Use these for real-life counting activities.
- Provide a wide range of hands-on counting experiences where the pupils have to count numbers that are not exact multiples of 10 or 100. The pupils will also need to be able to make the shift at the end of the counting sequence to include the extra ones left over, for example *10, 20, 30, 31, 32, 33, 34.* It is even more difficult to shift from 100s to 10s and then to 1s. For example, *100, 200, 300, 400, 500, 600, 700, 710, 720, 730, 731, 732, 733.*
- This is often a very challenging task and may need a lot of practice, so provide plenty of hands-on counting of large quantities of real objects.

- Use manipulative materials in school that lend themselves to grouping in 10s and 100s prior to introducing recording. Ensure that the children understand that these materials (popsticks grouped into bundles with elastic bands, Unifix cubes in sets of 10, etc) can stand as symbols for real objects.
- As well as asking pupils to count out quantities, ask them to set up and show you specific quantities. You can either use materials already packaged in tens or you can use loose items and get the pupils to group into tens and then count out: *Show me 140 buttons, show me 74 screws.* Ask them to count out as they do so, so that you can check that they are actually counting in 10s and not 1s!
- Get the pupils to use the 'copy and paste' function on the computer to produce patterns in multiples of ten.

◆◆◆◆◆◆◆◆◆◆   10

How did you get a line of ten? Did you insert the symbol ten times or could you copy and paste to do the job more quickly? What were some of the ways that you could make ten by copying and pasting?

◆◆◆◆◆◆◆◆◆◆
◆◆◆◆◆◆◆◆◆◆
◆◆◆◆◆◆◆◆◆◆   50
◆◆◆◆◆◆◆◆◆◆
◆◆◆◆◆◆◆◆◆◆

How did you make 50? Did you insert the symbol 50 times? Could you copy and paste to do the job more quickly? What are some of the different ways you can use copy and paste to get to 50?

◆◆◆◆◆◆◆◆◆◆
◆◆◆◆◆◆◆◆◆◆
◆◆◆◆◆◆◆◆◆◆
◆◆◆◆◆◆◆◆◆◆
◆◆◆◆◆◆◆◆◆◆   100
◆◆◆◆◆◆◆◆◆◆
◆◆◆◆◆◆◆◆◆◆
◆◆◆◆◆◆◆◆◆◆
◆◆◆◆◆◆◆◆◆◆
◆◆◆◆◆◆◆◆◆◆

How did you make 100? Did you insert the symbol 100 times? Could you copy and paste to do the job more quickly? What are some of the different ways you can use copy and paste to get to 100?

How would you use copy and paste to get to 1000 symbols?

- Play Reilly. Each pupil thinks of a number within a nominated range (for example any number between 20 and 80) and writes it down. One pupil is chosen as Reilly and his or her number becomes the target number and it is written on the board. Scoring is as follows:

If your number is exactly the same number as Reilly   100 points

If your number is within plus or minus 10 of Reilly   50 points

Repeat the process as many times as you like. Pupils keep their own scores. Obviously the winner is the pupil with the most points at the end of the game.

- Display a number line that extends to at least 1000 somewhere in your classroom and show the children how the 10s and 100s fall into a regular pattern in the sequence of numbers.
- Make opportunities for the children to work with large numbers. Measure out a 1000 metre running track. Look at the distances parents' or teachers' cars have travelled: *Whose car has traveled the furthest?*
- Look at maps and atlases. Find out how far it is to travel to different cities. *Who in the class would have to travel the furthest to visit their grandparents?*
- Look at world figures. *What is the population of India? Which country has the smallest population in the list that you are looking at? What is the population of your local town? How many people live in London?*
- Look at advertisements for expensive items like cars, boats and houses. Arrange them in order of price. *What could you buy if you had £10,000 or £500,000?*

Chapter 10

UNDERSTANDING PLACE VALUE IN WRITTEN NUMBERS

PLACE VALUE AND DYSCALCULIA

Learning to record numbers requires basic skills in being able to form numerals and remember the link between a spoken number and its written Arabic symbol. The base 10 system is highly efficient in using only nine numerals and a zero to represent any whole number in the number system: however, for pupils with dyscalculia there are some significant pitfalls.

> *One of the greatest difficulties for the pupil with dyscalculia is that written numbers seem to violate the* What you see is what you get *rule which applies in literacy. If you look at number 493 you might easily think that you have just got a four, a nine and a three. You cannot actually* see *the 400 or the 90.*

In using written numbers the pupil has to learn that a '2' can either represent the quantity 'two' or it can represent 'twenty', 'two hundred', 'two thousand' etc, depending on where it is positioned. There are no clues to tell you what you are looking at except the position of the 2 relative to the other numbers. The number 12 is different from 21 only because of the order in which the numbers are written.

The convention of working only in one direction (from left to right) does usually seem to apply to written numbers. However, the numbers between 13 and 19 seem to go against this rule.

> *The numbers 13–19 violate the rule on how to read printed symbols. In general the rule for saying numbers or reading words is the same. You follow the order in which the numbers or letters are printed: 43 is spoken as* forty three, cat *is read as* c-a-t. *However, with the numbers between 13 and 19 this rule does not apply, the last numeral is spoken first, for example* fourteen. *Many pupils with dyscalculia find this very confusing and take a long time to learn that you say* sixteen *and write 16.*

The concept of a number representing not only a single value but larger values as a multiples of 10, 100 or 1000 (*20 is 2 × 10, 200 is 2 × 100, 2000 is 2 × 1000*) demands that the child understands the basic principles of multiple addition or multiplication. They need to be able to conceptualise that 300 is 100 + 100 + 100 or 100 × 3.

Using base 10 seems to violate the rule of concrete counting each item only once. Items are counted with 1:1 correspondence but are then placed into groups of 10 (or 200, or 1000 etc) and then recounted. What you have just counted as 10 becomes 1 ten, *what you have just counted as 20 becomes* 2 tens.

Many pupils with difficulties in mathematics fail to understand that 0 does not represent 'nothing' but acts as a place holder. They reason that if 0 = nothing *then it can be ignored or discounted. From there it is difficult to understand the difference between 2, 20 and 200. If each is* two and nothing, *then don't all of these numbers really mean the same thing?*

Most children will learn to recognise some printed numbers without understanding the principles underlying the format. For example, they may be able to read 100, 99, 20 or other isolated numbers without being able to tell you why the numbers are written that way.

However, to be fully competent with written numbers, especially once they start using them in operations such as addition, they will need to understand place value.

Action plans for successful learning

- Before beginning to teach the system of reading and writing base 10 numbers, ensure that the pupils have become very comfortable in using base 10 in counting.
- It is always easier to recognise than to produce written symbols and so start with these. Make sure that the pupils are surrounded by written numbers and that informally they start to notice and recognise the written symbols that represent numbers.
- Encourage parents to make their children number aware. Look at the street numbers as you drive by, look at price tags, sports scores and the weather forecast. There is a parent information sheet at the end of this book that you can photocopy and give to parents.

- Use a number line to familiarise the children with double digit numbers.
- Get the children to arrange number cards in order following a sample number line.
- Use numbers in your surroundings (page numbers in books, house numbers etc) as one way of introducing double digit numbers to the children.
- Prepare a number line written on peel-off labels. Introduce counting activities above ten and ask the children to peel off the labels that they need to mark their quantities: *See, you have got fourteen, can you find the label for 14?*
- Get the children to make their own sets of tens (strings of beads, boxes of pencils, tubs of beans, bundles of popsticks etc). At first make sure that the tens are firmly grouped (in boxes, in bags, on strings, bound by elastic bands or connected together as Unifix, Lego blocks). It is a good idea for the children to colour code the containers or blocks: *red is for tens, ten pencils in a red box, ten red Lego blocks joined together.*

The ones are left loose and can be colour-coded by being placed on a coloured paper or decorated paper plate. The decorated paper plate can be used for a long time – it is very useful in early tens and units addition and subtraction as the 'home base' for the ones.

Work with boxes at first to show the pupils the importance of position and placement.

RED   BLUE

Tens	Ones
3	4

RED   BLUE

Tens	Ones
2	5

- Turn the task the other way around. Make number cards and ask the pupils to make the number shown on the cards with their manipulatives: *Show me 57, show me 29.*
- Teach the language of single units, they can be called *ones* or *units*.
- Prepare number cards with the decades on (10, 20, 30, 40 etc) and narrower cards with the single numbers (1, 2, 3, 4 etc). Show the pupils how to make new numbers by combining two of the cards: *We can make 36 by putting the 6 on top of the 30.* Give plenty of practice at making and reading numbers using these cards. Then introduce 100s using the same system. Remember to give the children practice with both creating *and* reading numbers made in this way.

Chapter 11

COMPOSITION AND DECOMPOSITION OF NUMBERS

DYSCALCULIA AND COMPOSITION AND DECOMPOSITION OF NUMBERS

That any number is a composite of other numbers is a key concept in mathematics. This idea underpins all computation and is essential if children are to learn to use the number system effectively.

Pupils with dyscalculia may understand the principle of this reasonably easily, but may find it hard to relate this knowledge to particular numbers. For instance, they may know that ten is a quantity in its own right. They will probably know that it can be decomposed into some smaller numbers. But they may have difficulty in knowing or remembering which particular numbers combine to make ten or exactly how ten is part of a larger number such as 18.

Nearly all pupils will have an intuitive awareness of some number patterns through early learning and play activities. For instance, most children will recognise a six on a dice without having to count. However, this will not necessarily mean that they understand the six that they recognise can also be described as *3 + 3* or *2 + 2 + 2*.

Halves and doubles of numbers are particularly useful in developing an understanding of the composition and decomposition of numbers. Being able to work with halves and doubles provides an important short cut to many mental calculations that will be required at a later stage. It is also a foundation concept for multiplication and division.

Understanding odd and even numbers is an important foundation for many mathematical skills. It allows for speedy counting in multiples of two, for the pupil to decide whether a number can be halved without a remainder, and for checking of answers using rules such as *an odd plus an even number always has an odd number answer.*

To understand fully and to apply the concept of composition and decomposition, pupils will need to be able to understand the four operations of addition, subtraction, division and multiplication. This is dealt with more fully in later chapters.

Action plans for successful learning

- Nominate a number and get the children to use real objects such as toy cars, pencils, shoes etc to create patterns of that number. Encourage them to explore all possible arrangements and then draw or photograph their arrangements for a permanent record. Talk about and record the permutations that the children have discovered.
- Get the children to use drawing, potato prints, dot paintings, stick-on shapes, collage or real objects to explore the number pattern(s) that can be associated with a particular number.
- Explore numbers with the children. Have a 'Number of the Week' and see how much you can all find out about that number. Draw patterns, arrange objects and explore in how many ways that number can be made.
- Get the children to make up their own charts to record composition and decomposition of the number as they discover the facts.

- Have a structured chart in the classroom that gives the basic composition and decomposition of numbers, which pupils with dyscalculia can refer to when they are working on mathematical problems.

1	2	3	4	5	6	7	8	9	10	11	12
1+0	1+1	1+2	1+3	1+4	1+5	1+6	1+7	1+8	1+9	1+10	1+11
	2+0	2+1	2+2	2+3	2+4	2+5	2+6	2+7	2+8	2+9	2+10
		3+0	3+1	3+2	3+3	3+4	3+5	3+6	3+7	3+8	3+9
			4+0	4+1	4+2	4+3	4+4	4+5	4+6	4+7	4+8
				5+0	5+1	5+2	5+3	5+4	5+5	5+6	5+7
					6+0	6+1	6+2	6+3	6+4	6+5	6+6
						7+0	7+1	7+2	7+3	7+4	7+5
							8+0	8+1	8+2	8+3	8+4
								9+0	9+1	9+2	9+3
									10+0	10+1	10+2
										11+0	11+1
											12+0
1	2	3	4	5	6	7	8	9	10	11	12

1	2	3	4	5	6	7	8	9	10	11	12
1-0	2-0	3-0	4-0	5-0	6-0	7-0	8-0	9-0	10-0	11-0	12-0
2-1	3-1	4-1	5-1	6-1	7-1	8-1	9-1	10-1	11-1	12-1	
3-2	4-2	5-2	6-2	7-2	8-2	9-2	10-2	11-2	12-2		
4-3	5-3	6-3	7-3	8-3	9-3	10-3	11-3	12-3			
5-4	6-4	7-4	8-4	9-4	10-4	11-4	12-4				
6-5	7-5	8-5	9-5	10-5	11-5	12-5					
7-6	8-6	9-6	10-6	11-6	12-6						
8-7	9-7	10-7	11-7	12-7							
9-8	10-8	11-8	12-8								
10-9	11-9	12-9									
11-10	12-10										
12-11											
1	2	3	4	5	6	7	8	9	10	11	12

- Cut out pictures of vehicles and mark how many people can fit into each. Prepare pictures or photographs of groups of people (photographs of the children in the class are great!). Put people in groups of between one and ten. Tell the children that all the people in each group want to stick together when they travel. *Which groups can travel in the car that takes five passengers? How can you fill up a minibus that takes 18 people without splitting up any groups?*
- Repeat the activity with larger numbers of people in each group and larger forms of transport. *How can you fill up the train carriage that seats 60 people?*
- Help pupils to improve their ability to recognise number patterns without counting. Prepare some cards with symmetrical and asymmetrical patterns and show them, one by one, to the children. Get the children to say how many items they see in each display. Gradually increase the number if items in the displays.
- To give children an understanding of *double,* put some items on the table and then use a mirror to create a reflection of the display. Count the items on the table and the images in the mirror and talk about how there is an exact duplicate in the mirror and so exactly twice as many items can be counted.
- Get the pupils to make a pattern of dots with paint on one half of a piece of paper. Fold the paper in half and open up. Count how many dots there are altogether. Double the number of dots because there is an exact duplicate of the original.
- Halving numbers is more difficult than doubling, because the pupil has to decide how to make the division between the two halves. The concept is often not fully understood until the child understands the operation of division. Making things a *fair share* helps the children to understand that halves have to be equal in number.
- Get the pupils to make patterns of numbers, giving them only even numbers: *Make me a pattern of eight dots, make me a pattern with six sticks.* Then repeat the activity with odd numbers: *Make me a pattern with seven shoes, make a pattern with five stars.* Talk to the pupils about the way the patterns work depending on whether they had the even numbers (usually symmetrical patterns) or odd numbers (usually asymmetrical patterns, uneven or 'odd').
- Introduce activities of sharing quantities into two sets. Get the children to record the results and talk about odds and evens.
- Use Lego blocks as one type of manipulative for discovering the unique properties of even numbers. *What happens if you count the dots on your Lego blocks? Can you ever get an odd number? What if you get an odd number of blocks, can you get an odd number of dots then?*
- Teach skip counting: *Say a number skip a number, say a number skip a number. Start by skipping one. Start by skipping two. Look at the pattern you make.*
- Practise counting even numbers in order. Practise counting odd numbers in order.
- Introduce activities of sharing quantities into two sets. Get the children to record the results and talk about odds and evens. *Look around you. What can you see that has an even pattern? What comes in pairs? What comes in an odd number?*

Chapter 12

ORDER OF MAGNITUDE OF NUMBERS AND THEIR RELATIONSHIP WITH EACH OTHER

ORDER OF MAGNITUDE AND DYSCALCULIA

The ability to understand the location of numbers relative to each other without any visual reference point is one of the most useful indicators of a child's aptitude for mathematical thinking.

Many children with dyscalculia have a significant deficit in this intuitive sense of number, because they lack an internal, abstract representation of the number system. While they may be able to count to quite large numbers, they can have significant difficulties in 'knowing' where a particular number is in the number system without physically seeing it in position.

> *Ishmael was excited about his new baby rabbits that had been born over the weekend.*
>
> *Ishmael:*   *And we got lots and lots of baby rabbits.*
>
> *Adult:*   *Do you know how many baby rabbits you've got?*
>
> *Ishmael:*   *Lots…I think there's 8…yes 8…or…or it might be 20.*
>
> *We can see that Ishmael has a poor sense of number. He thinks that the number of baby rabbits could be 8 or it could be 20, not realising that 20 is an improbable alternative to 8.*

Whereas other pupils may just 'know' that 20 is considerably larger than eight, the child with dyscalculia may need to work this out by mechanical counting or looking at a number line. This is a significant disadvantage in many areas of mathematics, especially in estimation where a poor 'feel' for numbers may allow silly errors in calculation to go unnoticed.

The child with dyscalculia may have a justified lack of confidence in their ability to estimate and may always use counting as a fail-safe method of getting the right answer.

Try this out with your pupils who have difficulties with mathematics.

Work in a room where there are no visible number lines. Ask questions like these:

What numbers come before and after 9?

What numbers come before and after 14?

What numbers come before and after 39?

What numbers come before and after 70?

What numbers come before and after 119?

Can they answer these questions automatically or do they need to work them out?

Do they need to count from one to find out the answers?

Do they count a partial sequence such as 35, 36, 37, 38, 39, 40?

Working out the number that comes before *the target number is often particularly difficult. Usually the pupil has to count to the target number and then backtrack to find the number that came* before.

The number that comes after *the target number is usually much easier but may still depend on counting.*

What does this tell us about the child's mental representation of the number sequence?

It tells us that the child's notion of the number system is still an external one, dependent on physical counting. They are not yet at the stage of 'knowing' the position of numbers relative to each other. They can move forwards in the counting sequence much more easily than they can move backwards. They often fail to use knowledge of the patterns of the number system to produce an answer without mechanical counting.

The ability to recognise relative magnitude of numbers is an essential foundation skill for estimation. It is important that children understand that, while counting is the most accurate way of telling 'how many', intuitive recognition and estimation are also important and legitimate mathematical skills.

A strong number sense is also an essential basis for efficient mathematical thinking and computation.

Action plans for successful learning

- To give practice in using a number line: write numbers on individual cards. Get your pupils to lay the cards out in the correct numerical order. They may need to work to a sample number line to start with.

Remove some of the numbers from the set, and replace them with blank cards. The pupils then have to lay the cards out, using blank cards, as substitutes for numbers which they do not have.

Give the pupils only a few numbers from the set, and ask them to lay them out in order of size (smallest to largest).

Get the pupils to lay about 6 cards out while blindfolded. As they are given each card they are told its number, their task is to put it down in the correct position relative to where they placed the other cards and relative to a hypothetical number line.

- Use sports scores to help pupils gain an appreciation of the way in which numbers relate to each other. Follow your local team and see how their scores compare with the competition. Have a league table for the season and keep a watch on how the teams or players move up or down in relation to others. Keep a watch on record times in athletics.
- Use a computer database to keep up-to-date sports information and print out graphs, bar charts, pie charts, and other ways of representing the data.
- Encourage estimation skills across the curriculum. *How many tadpoles do we have in the tank? How many boxes will we need to make our scenery for the class drama production? How many sandwiches will we need for the class picnic?*
- Give pupils mental exercises where they have to say numbers that come before and after a designated number: *What numbers come before and after 27?* Provide a written number line at first to help pupils find their way around the system.
- Talk to them about the patterns of numbers. Write the numbers down to show them how the final digits are in order: *26, 27, 28, see there's 6, 7, 8, so 26 comes before 27.*

- Handling numbers that end in 0, such as 20 or 300, need extra teaching. Give specific activities to encourage the pupils to think about the numbers that occur either side of a decade or a hundred.
- Page numbers in books and magazines help children to conceptualise the number sequence and what it actually means in practice. *Look at page numbers. Can you find the book which has the greatest number of pages? How quickly can you find a particular page number? Can you jump from one page number to another and be fairly accurate in knowing where to go? Can you tell me how to go from, say, page 83 to page 54, without having the book in their hands?* (A child who has a good understanding of the number system will be able to tell you, *Well, you have to go back … about 30 pages and then you will be quite close.*)
- Encourage children to use an index in a book (many children are fascinated to find how they can navigate their way through the book by using an index).
- Play Number King. One pupil is selected as the Number King and must think of a number. The other pupils must guess the number but can only ask *Is it bigger than …?* or *Is it smaller than …?* The Number King can only answer 'yes' or 'no'. The child who guesses the number becomes the next Number King.
- Play Hotter and Colder. One child thinks of a number, but can only answer 'Hotter' or 'Colder' as the other children guess what it is.
- Judge numbers by comparisons. In this activity the pupils are shown two similar sets of items (beads on strings, beans in jars, biscuits in a see-through box, etc). In each case one of the pair has a known quantity. The pupils are shown both sets of items and are asked, *This string has eight beads on it. How many beads do*

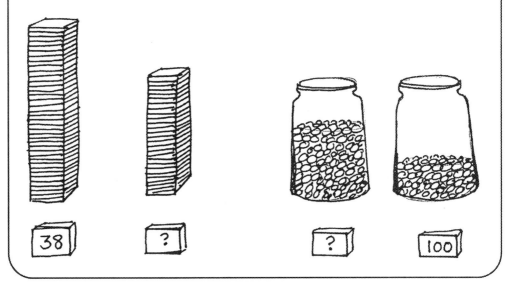

you think the other string has? This jar has 22 beans in it, how many beans do you think the other jar contains?

- Encourage the pupils to estimate and judge rather than to actually count. Once estimates have been made then they can check by counting.
- Repeat the above activity but base it on pictures rather than real objects. Make work cards where the pupils have to estimate and not count items.

UNDERSTANDING OPERATIONS

Understanding the four operations (addition, subtraction, multiplication and division) is of course an absolute fundamental of the mathematics curriculum. For pupils with learning disorders, getting to grips with the underlying processes can be one of the major hurdles in their acquisition of basic mathematical skills.

Chapter 13

DYSCALCULIA AND OPERATIONS

It has been said that understanding the number system is the mathematical equivalent to having good phonological awareness in literacy. To be able to read and spell well, the pupil needs to understand the way in which spoken words are made up of sounds that can be manipulated to make sense. In order to understand the four operations (and other mathematical concepts), the pupil has to be able to understand the number system as a starting point.

Unfortunately, children are often introduced to algorithms far too early, before they understand the fundamentals of the number system. This is a recipe for long-term mathematical difficulties, as the more advanced concepts of the four operations will be based on inadequate understanding of the basic concepts.

The pupil with dyscalculia may have very limited understanding of the way in which the number system can be manipulated in a systematic way to add, subtract, multiply and divide.

We need to remember that our young learners are coming to mathematics from the preliminary stages of literacy learning. What have they learned through reading and writing skills?

- Always read and write from left to right.
- *What you see is what you get* rule applies. If you see *c-a-t* you have to say *c-a-t.*
- The sentences that you are given to read are usually complete and mean something.
- The sentences that you read could end differently but still make sense.
- No action is required from you to complete what you see in front of you.

Although we often tell children that they are working on 'number sentences', these new sentences seem to behave quite differently from the familiar written sentences. With the introduction of mathematical operations the ground rules for dealing with 'sentences' shift in radical ways:

- Early number sentences are set out from left to right, later they are arranged vertically.
- The *What you see is what you get* rule does not always apply. If you see $6 - 4$, 4×5 or $10 - 2$ you do not actually *have* a tangible 4, 5 or 2.

- You always have to *do* something with the numbers in the number sentence.
- The number sentences are often incomplete, you have to finish them off yourself.
- The number sentences can only end in one way.
- Number sentences are made up of two statements that have to balance each other.

These fundamentals are often very confusing for the pupil with dyscalculia. Indeed dyscalculia literally means 'a difficulty with calculation'. The processes required in addition, subtraction, multiplication and division are complex. The child with a poor grasp of the number system is likely to find the interrelationship between the numbers and the operations totally mysterious.

> *We continued to toil every day, not only at letters but at words, and also at what was much worse, figures.*
>
> *Letters after all had only got to be known, and when they stood together in a certain way one recognised their formation and that it meant a certain sound or word which one uttered when pressed sufficiently.*
>
> *But the figures were tied into all sorts of tangles and did things to one another which it was extremely difficult to forecast with complete accuracy. You had to say what they did each time they were tied up together and the Governess attached enormous importance to the answer being exact. If it was not right then it was wrong. It was not any use being 'nearly right'. In some cases these figures got into debt with one another: you had to borrow one or carry one, and afterwards pay back the one you had borrowed. These complications cast a steadily gathering shadow over my daily life.*
>
> *They took one away from all the interesting things ... they became a general worry and preoccupation. More especially this was true when we descended into a dismal bog called 'sums'. There appeared to be no limit to these. When one sum was done there was always another. Just as soon as I managed to tackle a particular class of these afflictions, some other much more variegated type was thrust upon me.*
>
> *Winston Churchill,* My Early Life

Chapter 14

UNDERSTANDING ALGORITHMS

Just as the pupil will have already learned important conventions about reading and writing printed words, they will now have to learn the special conventions that relate to recording the four operations.

There is a very special code that is used. As adults we tend to take $2 + 3 = 5$ or $6 \times 5 = 30$ for granted, but to the young pupil there are some hidden rules that need to be understood before any progress in understanding can be made.

The pupil will be introduced to a new type of symbol. These symbols are part of the specialist language the pupil will learn as part of their mathematical development.

The symbols themselves are novel, geometric forms quite different to the letters and words that the child will have been working with in literacy:

- *Single shapes (not sequences of letters) are used to represent a spoken word.*

- *The same symbol can represent several, different words:* $+$ *can mean* add *or* plus, $-$ *can mean* take away *or* minus.

- *Actions can be physical and/or mental.*

Many young learners treat mathematical symbols as an extension of the literacy symbols they are learning. They then misunderstand algorithms and see them as a concrete representation of a set of numbers, in the same way that printed letters stand for spoken words. Pupils often need to be shown how to 'crack the code' of the algorithm and to understand the operation that it describes can be performed physically or mentally.

The concept of equivalence also needs to be taught, and the sign $=$ needs to be introduced as a symbol with its own specific meaning. Children with dyscalculia often have difficulties with the language, and *equals* may be unfamiliar to them. You will remember the child in Chapter 2 who thought that $=$ meant *eagles*.

Action plans for successful learning

- Ensure that the pupil has a very firm grasp of the number system before you attempt to introduce algorithms.
- Always introduce symbols and algorithms as a means of recording real mathematical actions. Start with the action and then teach how to record what you have done: *We had ten fish but we have given six to Mr Jenkins and now we have four left. How can we write this down so we can remember? We can write 10 − 6 = 4. What can we write for Mr Jenkins? He already had two fish. So we can write 2 + 4 = 6.*
- Teach each new symbol very carefully. Keep your vocabulary consistent at first to avoid confusion, for example use either *add* or *plus* at first, not both.
- Give explicit instruction about mathematical synonyms: *Add means the same as plus, take away means the same as subtract.*
- Train parents to use the same mathematical language as you.
- Give and take (an addition and subtraction activity).

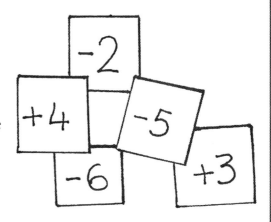

Make a set of cards each with a + or − sign and a number, for example 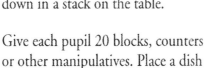 Place the cards, face down in a stack on the table.

Give each pupil 20 blocks, counters or other manipulatives. Place a dish with extra blocks in the centre of the table. Each child takes a card from the pile and follows the operation on the card. If they have a + card they take the extra blocks from the dish. If they have a − card they take blocks from their set and place them in the dish. The winner is the first person to get rid of all their blocks. (It helps if there are slightly more cards with a minus sign on them.)

For a small group of more capable pupils you can ask them to record the operations. They start with 20 and each time they add or take away on the record.

$$20$$
$$20 + 3 = 23$$
$$23 - 7 = 16$$
$$16 - 9 = 7$$
$$7 + 3 = 10$$
$$10 - 5 = 5$$
$$5 + 4 = 9$$
$$9 - 9 = 0$$

- Teach the concept of equivalence and the use of the = sign. Set up activities where the children use cards with = and ≠ to make displays that illustrate the concept of equivalence and non equivalence:

  2 flowers in a vase = 2 flowers in a vase, 6 apples in a bowl ≠ 3 apples in a bowl.

- Give explicit instruction so that the pupils really do understand what the setting out of an algorithm actually represents.

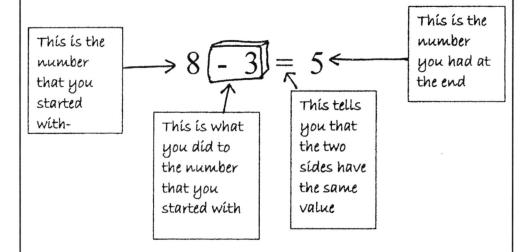

- It is particularly important that the child understands that the symbol (+, −, × or ÷) and the number that follows it work together (like a code) to indicate an operation.

Encourage the pupil to draw around the sign and the number that follows it, to identify the operation that they are doing. You can call these small segments of the algorithm *job cards* to make it easier for the pupil to remember and follow through with the correct process.

Turn the sequence of numbers and symbols into everyday language: *The job is to take away 2* or *the job is to add on 6.* This helps minimise the pupil's tendency to treat all numbers in the algorithm as concrete numbers.

- Show and tell (an addition, subtraction, multiplication and division activity).

$$4 \boxed{+ 3} =$$

the job is to add on 3

$$6 \boxed{- 2} =$$

the job is to take away 2

Pupils need a lot of practice in understanding and implementing simple algorithms associated with the four operations. Working in a group and watching others make their patterns and discussing the results with a supportive adult is a good way to build confidence in 'reading' the mathematical sentences they are given.

Set pupils up with a supply of manipulatives. It is important to use a range, so that the pupils do not simply 'lock on' to the idea that an operation is only performed with (say) counters or popsticks.

Prepare a set of flashcards, covering the four algorithms. The pupils have to look at the algorithm and 'show and tell'. They look at the algorithm, and they then arrange their materials so that they can demonstrate the algorithm.

A pupil might, for instance, put together three red blocks + four blue blocks before they 'tell' that $3 + 4 = 7$, or six rows of four before they 'tell' that $6 \times 4 = 24$.

With subtraction an additional piece of equipment is required. The pupil needs a small box, a piece of paper etc, which can cover up some of their display. They set out their materials and then obscure the number which they are to subtract. As they 'tell' they place their shield over the items that they are subtracting. *Six* (place shield over two items) *take away 2 is 4.*

In division they set out their manipulatives to reflect the division operation that they have completed: $12 \div 3 = 4$ is displayed as three groups of four manipulatives.

• The order in which the operations may (or may not) be done needs to be understood and remembered. While addition and multiplication are reversible, subtraction and division are not.

Some children are helped by the mnemonic:

+ and × have *two* lines in the symbol. You can do the calculation *two* ways to produce the same answer (2 + 3 or 3 + 2, 4 × 5 or 5 × 4, it does not matter).

− and ÷ have only *one* line in the symbol. You can only do the operation *one* way [6 − 3 but not 3 − 6, 12 ÷ 3 but not 3 ÷ 12).

• Prove it! (an addition and subtraction activity)

In this activity the pupils are shown a completed algorithm (which may or may not be correct) and asked to 'prove it'. For example, the adult writes *5 + 6 = 11* or *8 − 3 = 6.*

Each child in the group has to set up manipulatives (counters, popsticks, shells etc) to prove that the algorithm is correct or incorrect. They have to give a verbal justification of their proof: *See, I got five shells and then I got six shells and then I counted 11, so it is right!* Or *Well, I took eight blocks and took three away and there's only five left, so the card is wrong, it's not six, it's five. Five is the right answer.*

Chapter 15

ADDITION

The + sign is usually the one that most children recognise and use most comfortably. Addition is the most concrete of the four operations and it is usually taught first.

Some pupils with dyscalculia may find learning the symbol-name association difficult, especially if different words (*add, plus, add up, sum,* and) are used interchangeably in association with the + sign. However, algorithms using + are usually solid concrete actions. Two tangible quantities are combined together to make a total.

Addition is the only operation where the *What you see is what you get* rule always applies. If you have 3 + 4 then you actually have three visible, tangible items and you have four visible, tangible items, which is just what you would expect from what you see on the paper.

However, even here things are not that simple. To get the answer you have to re-use the 3 and the 4 to create the new number (7). In creating the 7 you may have lost sight of the 3 and the 4 that you started with.

If you understand the composition and decomposition of numbers, then this is not a problem. If you do not really understand that the number 7 can be decomposed into 3 + 4 then you may simply 'do' the sum mechanically without it making much sense at all.

The ability to visualise makes a substantial contribution to being able to 'see' the two smaller quantities composed into the larger one. Unfortunately pupils with dyscalculia often have significant deficits in visualisation skills.

They frequently have a limited understanding of the composition/decomposition rules that apply to addition, and so find it hard to understand the commutative principle (*if 3 + 4 = 7 then 4 + 3 also = 7*). Nor will they necessarily understand that subtraction is a reversal of the addition process (*7 − 4 = 3, 7 − 3 = 4*).

(STRATEGIES)

There are various strategies that children use to solve addition algorithms. These strategies range from concrete to abstract.

Strategy	Process to solve 3 + 4
Count each and then count all	1 2 3 . . . . . 1 2 3 4 . . . . . 1 2 3 4 5 6 7
Count all	1 2 3 4 5 6 7
Count on from the first addend	3 . . . . . 4 5 6 7
Count on from the larger addend	4 . . . . . 5 6 7
Linking known facts	3 + 3 = 6, + 1 more = 7
Retrieving the number fact	7

Pupils with dyscalculia generally have very poor retention of number facts. This means that they cannot use the more advanced strategies of linking known facts or retrieving known facts when working with addition. This is a problem when adding single digits and a major hurdle when dealing with larger numbers.

Many children who have difficulties recalling number facts do eventually remember some of the basics. However, they often fail to tap in to this existing knowledge base, and always resort to concrete counting. Perhaps it is easier always to count than to stop and think, *Do I know this one?*

Many children with dyscalculia persist in the very concrete 'count each and count all' addition strategy. At first they may use manipulatives and then start using their fingers or tally marks.

The use of tally marks is a very useful transition strategy bridging the gap between counting tangible objects to mental computation. For the child with dyscalculia, tally marks are often a vital lifeline. However, tally marks are often used inefficiently. The child may spend a considerable proportion of their mathematics lesson making tally marks and then counting and recounting them, often several times over. They will often draw a fresh set of tally marks for each calculation, even when they have already got tally marks for the numbers that they need.

The use of fingers in computation is widespread. Many adults use their fingers in some circumstances, for example when working out dates or simple totals. Pupils with dyscalculia may depend on their fingers for counting as a compensation for having poor recall of number facts and poor computation/reasoning skills. Unfortunately many children with dyscalculia have difficulties in working with their fingers. Often they make systematic errors, such as counting the same finger twice, or they get spatially confused with where they are with their fingers and the counting process.

'Counting on' is an important skill for addition when number facts are not known automatically. This is an area when pupils with dyscalculia can often make particularly good headway, provided they have explicit teaching in the technique and sufficient practice using it.

Mental manipulation of number facts, even when the facts are known or provided for them, can prove to be very difficult indeed for the child with dyscalculia. Indeed, such difficulties are used to diagnose the condition. However, it is also probably true to say many children feel overwhelmed by their initial difficulties with mental computation. They may then choose to rely on the safer, more tangible strategies for addition and never attempt to venture into mental computation.

Action plans for successful learning

- Refer back to the chart on strategies for addition and evaluate the pupil's current strategy when they add two single digits together. You may find that there is scope for explicit teaching of more advanced counting strategies such as the effective use of tally marks, and adding strategies such as counting on.
- Pupils with dyscalculia often have prolonged difficulty with learning and retaining number facts.
- Some children who know a few number facts may choose always to use concrete counting in preference to having to stop and think about whether a number fact is known or not. Before the pupils start an addition exercise, get them to go through the sheet and mark any number facts that they *know they know* with a highlighter pen. Encourage them to go straight to the answer on these items without counting.
- The pupil may need to use a chart of number facts and/or a calculator as a long-term solution to their difficulties with number fact recall. If so, these resources should be provided without question, and you should give instructions on their correct use.

- Count on us (a counting on activity for 2–6 players).

Put plenty of buttons (or any other manipulatives) in the middle of the table. The aim of this game is to work out how many buttons the whole group has between them.

Each child takes a handful of buttons from the central supply without counting. The first child counts his or her buttons and says the final number clearly. The next child picks up the counting sequence and counts his or her buttons. The counting continues around the table until the final child completes the counting sequence.

- Button up (a counting on activity)

You need some strips of firm card, with buttons sewn on. The buttons are sewn on in a row and the number of buttons is marked clearly at the end of the card. There should be between one and nine buttons on each card.

The pupil has two button cards. They are asked to say how many buttons they have altogether. They must say the number of buttons on the first card (without counting), and then count on the buttons on the second card: *6 ... 7, 8, 9, 10.*

Once they can do this they should be shown how to do it faster by always choosing the card with the most buttons on as their first card, so that they have the least number of buttons left to count.

- If the pupil uses a number line to support counting, give explicit instruction and guided practice on using 'counting on' rather than 'counting all'.
- If a pupil is using tally marks inefficiently (for instance, constantly making new sets of tally marks for every calculation), provide them with a tally mark chart (or get them to make their own) so that they have simple, organised set of symbols to count. This can be reused time and time again.

●	1
● ●	2
● ● ●	3
● ● ● ●	4
● ● ● ● ●	5
● ● ● ● ● ●	6
● ● ● ● ● ● ●	7
● ● ● ● ● ● ● ●	8
● ● ● ● ● ● ● ● ●	9
● ● ● ● ● ● ● ● ● ●	10

- Instead of using tally marks for both numbers, teach the pupils to write down one number. They can then use tally marks and count on the second number.

$$6 + 3 = 9$$

6 |||

$$2 + 7 = 9$$

7 ||

- It is better still if the pupil can draw a line under the largest number, make tally marks for the smallest and then use counting on from the largest number to get their answer.

$$\underline{8} + 2 = 10$$

||

$$3 + \underline{5} = 8$$

|||

- Explicitly teach the pupil the short cut of always using the larger number as the starting point for counting on.
- If they do draw their own tally marks as they work, encourage them to organise their tally marks in orderly rows to facilitate accurate counting.

  - Teach mental manipulation of numbers in gradual stages so that pupils with difficulties do not feel overwhelmed.
  - When you are confident that your pupils know the doubles for all single digits teach them how to use this knowledge for mental addition.

Make up some cards with addition algorithms where there is only a difference of one between the numbers on the cards, for example 6 + 7 5 + 4 7 + 8

Ask the children to spot the difference between the numbers (you have made it easy by only having a difference of one).

Then show them how they have easier calculations to do, $6 + 6 + 1$ or $4 + 4 + 1$ etc. When they can do this introduce pairs of numbers that have a difference of two and repeat the activity. Gradually add in more differences as they gain confidence.

- Using tens in mental computation. First, choose a pair of numbers that add up to 10 (for example, $6 + 4$). You are only using one number pair in order to make it really clear and straightforward for the pupils.

Prepare a set of single and double digit numbers, taking care that all the numbers end in 6 or 4.

Then make some other number cards, but this time make sure that there are no pairs that could combine to make a multiple of 10. These cards are just the 'fillers' used to help the pupils to concentrate on looking for the specific number pair that you have chosen.

Example:

| 6 | | 14 | | 29 | | 17 | | 4 | | 25 | | 16 | | 38 | | 34 | | 7 | | 16 |

Spread all the cards on the table, mixing the cards that end in 6 or 4 with the 'fillers'. Remind the pupils of the number fact *6 + 4 = 10*. The pupils then see how many pairs of cards they can make where they can utilise their knowledge of *6 + 4 = 10*. Show them how they can now mentally calculate *6 + 14, 16 + 34* or *14 + 16* etc.

Repeat the activity with other number pairs, making sure that you target only one pair at a time to simplify the process.

USING VERTICAL SETTING OUT

Many pupils with dyscalculia have not mastered addition of two single digits before they are moved on to the addition of larger numbers. If this occurs then the child faces a very difficult and frustrating challenge, as they will be using immature and inefficient counting strategies to deal with these more complex calculations.

Vertical setting out of double digit addition involves a shift from horizontal *8 + 1 = 9* to vertical, and the introduction of place value. It is obviously of critical importance that the children understand place value before they start to work with addition using tens and units and beyond. You will find further information on place value in Chapter 10.

It is useful to start pupils off using the correct order of operations and direction of working for even the easiest of calculations, so that they develop good working habits right from the start.

The young learner may have just grasped the concept of working from left to right in reading and writing the →cat→sat→on→the→mat.

They have successfully transferred this new habit to mathematics, working from left to right in 2→+ 4=→6.

However, once they are working vertically the direction of operations changes to right to left as they learn to deal with the 'ones' before the 'tens'.

Think about how the pupil has to record the 15 in this additional sum.

Do they work from right to left, or left to right? Do they write 1 and then 5 (in that order)? Or do they write 5 (in the ones column) and then place a 1 in the tens column afterward which means they are writing the number 15 'backwards'?

$$38$$
$$\overset{1}{5}7$$
$$\overline{1\ 85}$$

Where do they put the 1 in the tens column? In this example the child believes a new '15' has been created in the tens column. They have shown their working, 8 + 7 = 15, 15 + 3 = 18.

What are the demands on their spatial awareness in doing this, apparently simple, operation?

$$8+7=15$$

$$15+3=18$$

The process of regrouping units to form tens should be well understood before formal operations with paper and pencil are expected of the pupil. Many children do not really understand what they are doing with the columns of figures and just 'number crunch'.

In the example on the previous page the pupil has followed the correct system for the units column (although we might wonder if he understood what he was doing!) but has not understood that the one 10 that he has transferred creates only six tens, and not 15 tens as he has assumed.

Action plans for successful learning

- Watch pupils work with manipulatives and see if they can regroup units (ones) to form tens. Check that they can show you how to make a number such as 27 using manipulatives by forming two groups of 10 and 7 ones. If they cannot, then give further instruction and guided practice before expecting them to add double digit numbers or regroup in tens and units addition.
- Children who have mastered basic horizontal addition do not usually have much trouble with vertical addition until regrouping of units is required.
- Give direct instruction to enable pupils to understand that the vertical addition follows the same rules as the horizontal addition. They can use number facts that they know or they can count on to find a total.
- Ensure that the pupils understand the correct order and direction of working. Always start at the top of the sum. That is the number that you begin with. The lower number and its sign are the instructions that you have to follow. You might continue to use the *job card system* that was described on page 86.
- When first introducing addition with regrouping of units, return to the same materials that were used in teaching base 10. Set up the tens and units in a physical form and allow the children to manipulate the materials. They work out the total for the units' column, building a new 10 if necessary and transferring it over to join the other 10s that are already made up. The pupils then record their answer.

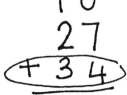

the job is to add 34 to 27

Use *Show and tell* cards to get the pupil to work though tens and units addition at a very practical level with a supportive adult.

Show me	24	Show me	29
Add on +	12	Add on +	14
How many now?		How many now?	

Make sure that they add the units and then the tens. Show them how to record the 10 that is transferred from the units to the tens column.

- Always encourage the pupils to estimate the answer they expect to get before they begin their calculation. Show them how to do a quick total of the tens column – their answer will never be more than one decade above that total.

- Get the pupils to make themselves a chart or poster to give them a rough guide to what answers to expect when they add tens and units. For instance, they might make a chart of addition facts in tens. If their chart tells them that *60 + 60 = 120* then they can estimate that 57 + 56 will be slightly less than 120.

Chapter 16

SUBTRACTION

The subtraction sign is usually a simple one to recognise, although varying vocabulary can cause a lot of confusion: *take away, minus, subtract, less.*

> *Jess looked at* 6 – 4 *and asked,* Is this take away or minus?

This is probably the first situation where the pupil has to deal with a number sentence where only one of the numbers on the page represents a visible, tangible quantity. The *What you see is what you get* rule does not seem to apply.

The second number only exists as an integral part of the first number given. Jess cannot follow the number sentence and physically set out six blocks and then four blocks. She has to realise that she does not have to deal with two separate numbers (6 and 4). In fact she only has one number (6) and has to withdraw the 4 from it.

To understand this she has to understand composition and decomposition of numbers. If she understands that 6 is made up of 4 + 2 she will also be able to understand that it is possible to remove or *take away* the 4, leaving the 2 behind. This is significantly more abstract than adding two tangible quantities together.

STRATEGIES

Strategy	Process to solve $8 - 6$
Count all, count back to subtract	1, 2, 3, 4, 5, 6, 7, 8, . . . 7, 6, 5, 4, 3, 2
Count back from the largest number	7, 6, 5, 4, 3, 2
Count up from the lowest number	7, 8
Link known facts	$8 - 4 = 4, 4 - 2 = 2, 6 + 2 = 8$, so $8 - 6 = 2$
Retrieve the number fact	2

Pupils with dyscalculia often find the process of counting in reverse very difficult because they easily lose track of the sequence. They will usually be very dependent on manipulatives or tally marks to keep themselves on track. Their use of tally marks may be inefficient.

Although the pupils may not have good recall of many number facts, they may know a few, especially addition facts. However, they often fail to draw on this existing knowledge to help with subtraction. They may know *6 + 2 = 8* but not use this knowledge to help them with *8 − 6*.

Action plans for successful learning

- Ensure that the pupils have plenty of practice in linking subtraction algorithms with hands-on subtraction using manipulatives.
- Use the *job card* described in the section on Understanding Algorithms (see page 86) to clarify what they are supposed to be doing. The sign in combination with the second number tell you what to do: $\boxed{6-4}$ *tells you that you start with 6. The job is to take 4 away.*
- Use a standard number line. Give the pupil subtraction algorithms – $\boxed{12-6}$, $\boxed{9-3}$, $\boxed{15-12}$ – and show them how to count up (not back) to find the difference between the two numbers. (Counting up is much easier for all children, especially those with dyscalculia.)
- Recognising differences in pairs of numbers. Make cards with pairs of numbers. At first make the difference between each item in a pair no greater than three. The child has to sort the cards into sets according to the difference between the two numbers.

Difference of 1	**Difference of 2**	**Difference of 3**

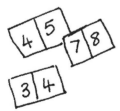  

Once the pupil handles these easily, introduce bigger differences between the numbers using the same method.

- Happy Families (a game to build familiarity with complementary and commutative number facts). Every number fact has three 'relatives'. Addition

---

facts are reversible so that $3 + 4$ can be reversed to $4 + 3$. There are also two complementary subtraction facts: $7 - 3$ and $7 - 4$.

Make a set of cards along the lines of 'Happy Families'. The 'families' are sets of four related number facts. The cards are shuffled and then each player takes a card in turn. Players take one card in each round. The players collect 'families' and the person with the most completed families wins.

USING VERTICAL SETTING OUT

The pupil with dyscalculia often finds this particularly confusing. Once again there is often a real problem in understanding that they only have one number (the number at the top of the sum) and that the subtraction sign in combination with the lower number is an instruction on what to do and not a number in its own right.

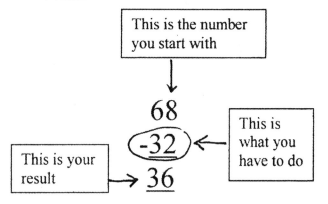

A major difficulty is the problem of the direction of working. Many pupils who are faced with two numbers will simply take the smaller number from the larger regardless of position. Sometimes they get away with it and sometimes they do not!

This type of subtraction usually brings with it the first experience in mathematics of an apparently impossible task: *Six from four you can't do.*

Never before has the child been given a sum that cannot be done! It's a shame that such an abstract concept is usually embedded in an already challenging task the very first time it is encountered. Not only is the pupil grappling with two double digit numbers and subtraction, now they have to get to grips with the fact that there are some apparently impossible operations! The solution to the problem is also introduced within the context of an already difficult process for the young learner.

It is essential that the pupil can demonstrate a clear understanding of the way in which a *ten* can be decomposed to provide *ones* before they can be expected to understand subtraction where exchanging is required.

Action plans for successful learning

- Well before double digit subtraction is introduced, give the pupils experience in subtracting where they get into negative territory. Set up activities where the children are working with manipulatives and discover that sometimes the subtraction algorithms will not work with the items they have been given. They will discover that the only way around the problem is to borrow from a friend or open a new box of manipulatives! Teach them to decompose tens at this stage before they have to try to handle the more abstract challenges of a written sum.
- When tens and units subtraction is first introduced, make sure that the children have the same manipulatives that they used when working on place value. Show them how to use the manipulatives to work through the process.

Make sure that they set themselves up with only one set of manipulatives to represent the top number in the sum (many will want to get a second set of manipulatives to represent the other set of numbers). Then give them a lot of guided practice in removing the required quantity from that amount.

- Use *Show and tell* cards to get the pupils to work through tens and units subtraction at a very practical level with a supportive adult:

Show me	28
Take away —	12
How many left?	

Show me	23
Take away —	18
How many left?	

Check that they do not use one-by-one subtraction, but deal with the units first and then the tens.

- When exchanging is required, make sure that manipulatives are used to assist in making the exchange. Children need to see how to physically decompose a ten to make sufficient units for the process of subtraction to continue successfully. This needs to be carefully taught and thoroughly practiced.
- The recording method must be taught in conjunction with the physical manipulation of the materials so that the pupils really understand what they are doing and why.
- Give to the poor (a game to practise decomposition).

You need a stack of cards with single and double digit numbers on. You will need about 20 cards per team.

Set up the children in groups of three. You will need two or more teams. Each team has 99 Unifix cubes (9 tens and 9 ones).

One child in each team is called King of Tens. He or she is in charge of the tens and starts off with 90 Unifix cubes, which must be joined together in tens.

The second child is called King of Ones. He or she is in charge of the single Unifix blocks and starts off with nine of them. These are loose in an open container.

The King of Tens and the King of Ones are seated side by side at a desk with their supplies of cubes in front of them. The third child is the runner.

At the starter's signal the runner runs to the stack of cards, takes one card, runs back to their team and says the number of tens and ones needed: *I need 2 tens and 4 ones.* They must always go to the King of Ones first. They must then go to the King of Tens if they need tens.

Sooner or later the King of Ones will run out of cubes. They must then turn to the King of Tens and say:

I need some more
To give to the poor.

The King of Tens gives a ten to the King of Ones. The ten is broken up into individual cubes and the runner is given the number of single cubes that they require. The King of Tens then gives the runner any complete tens needed. The runner races back and drops the cubes into a bucket and gets another card.

The team that gets rid of their 99 cubes first is the winner. The teacher can ask the King of Tens and King of Ones to record their declining number of cubes and/or can use the game as a teaching opportunity for decomposition of 10 in subtraction.

• Recognise that for many pupils with dyscalculia, the process of subtraction of large numbers (especially when exchanging and decomposition is required) may be very difficult and frustrating. Be prepared to provide a number square and/or calculator to enable the pupil to progress with problem solving and mathematical reasoning even if they have trouble with the mechanical process of subtraction.

Chapter 17

MULTIPLICATION

Multiplication is most easily understood as repeated addition, although unlike addition, one of the numbers in the algorithm is not a tangible quantity, but part of the code that tells the child what operation to perform. For instance, 3×4 tells us that the job is to add three, four times over: *3 + 3 + 3 + 3.*

Many pupils still follow the *What you see is what you get* rule and treat a multiplication algorithm as if it required addition. Shown *3 × 4* they see the numbers 3 and 4 and make the assumption that they are dealing with two concrete quantities and so 'number crunch' the two numbers together. They produce 7 as their answer.

Pupils with language-related learning difficulties often become very confused about the term 'times' when this is applied to multiplication. For many of them, their understanding of the word relates to *time* as in seconds, minutes and hours.

The $\times$ sign often causes confusion to the child with dyscalculia. It looks very similar to $+$, and if the child has visuospatial difficulties the two symbols may be confused.

Although multiplication is really repeated addition it is, of course, treated as a different operation because the tedious process of repeated addition can be circumvented by the use of multiplication facts. This means that there are a lot of multiplication facts to be learned and for the pupil with dyscalculia this can be a very daunting, if not impossible prospect.

Action plans for successful learning

- Pupils need to be introduced to the notion of performing an action, a specified number of times over:
  Jump × 6
  Clap × 4
  I want you to do three dots × 3
  I want you to draw two pigs × 5
  Show me five counters × 2

- Experiment with patterns (potato prints, stamps, stickers etc) to explore the patterns of multiplication and record the number facts that are discovered in this way.
- Many children can see that ✗ is like + rolling along. As it rolls over and over so the addition is repeated time and time again! The number that follows the ✗ tells you how many times you have to make the first number 'roll over'. Use this concept as a prompt to link the sign with the process.
- Use *Show and Tell* cards to help pupils to understand what a multiplication algorithm really means.

Show me 6	• • • • • •	Show me 5	• • • • •
Show me 6 x 5		Show me 5 x 3	
How many now?	30	How many now?	15

- Get the children to build up their own number square of multiplication facts. They will have a better understanding if they have made it for themselves. Start with a simple chart where they only deal with the numbers 1 to 4, so that the largest multiplication fact they have on their chart is *4 ✗ 4 = 16*. Gradually introduce bigger squares: 5 ✗ 5 where the largest number is 25, then 6 ✗ 6 where the largest number is 36, and so on.

	1	2	3	4
1	1	2	3	4
2	2	4	6	8
3	3	6	9	12
4	4	8	12	16

- For the pupil with dyscalculia, learning all of the tables may be impossible, or take an unreasonable amount of time and effort. In this case it is better to concentrate on a few key multiplication facts and then use a calculator for the rest.
- Long mulitplication is a multi-step process that many pupils find confusing. It should not be introduced until the child knows their multiplication facts well or can use a number square efficiently. They must also be very comfortable with place value and regrouping in addition. Always provide a step-by-step guide for those children who find it hard to remember the sequence of operations.

Chapter 18

DIVISION

Division is the most abstract of the four operations and many pupils with dyscalculia find it a very difficult concept. Looking at the *12 ÷ 3* they will often see the − sign, assume it is subtraction and use their understanding of decomposition, to produce the answer 9.

Division can be presented as repeated subtraction, which is the reverse of multiplication. This is the most concrete and more easily understood approach. It also helps to emphasise the link between multiplication and division. Once multiplication and its link with division is understood then division itself should be relatively easy to teach.

Division can also be taught as a process of equal sharing. This is a more abstract approach and is usually a more difficult concept/process for the child with dyscalculia to master. For instance, it is fairly easy to calculate 650 ÷ 50 by repeated subtraction, but much harder to work it out by equal sharing using the *one for you, one for you, one for you* method.

As with the other three operations, it is essential that pupils have an understanding of the basic number system, especially the compound nature of numbers, before they can begin to understand division, however it is introduced.

Most children with dyscalculia will need far more foundation work in the number system than their peers before they will be comfortable with the concept and process of division.

The child's difficulties are not helped by the fact that division can be presented in several different ways, each with its different working method.

$$12 \div 3 \qquad 3\overline{)12} \qquad \frac{12}{3}$$

Various words are used to refer to the process of division: *share between, divide, between, into.*

Action plans for successful learning

- Check that the pupil understands the concepts of multiplication and subtraction before introducing division. If they do then the basic concepts and processes of division should be fairly readily understood.
- Always start with real-life examples of the process of division, so that the pupils understand how the process relates to real life. *We have 28 children who need to get to the swimming carnival, and each parent can take 4 children in their car. So how many cars will we need? We can write this down as 28 ÷ 4 = .* Find as many practical examples as you can and demonstrate to the pupils the way in which the process is recorded.
- Start with repeated subtraction and when that is mastered, teach equal sharing as an alternative method of division. Use manipulatives and guided practice, so that you monitor the pupil as they follow through the algorithms with physical action.

20 ÷ 4 [repeated subtraction]	
Show me	20
Take away 4 over and over again	
How many times could you take 4 away?	5

20 ÷ 4 [equal sharing]	
Show me	20
Share it between 4 plates	
How many on each plate?	5

- The ÷ sign can also be taught as a 'special' sort of subtraction, where the dots remind you to keep taking away until you have nothing left.
- The ÷ sign can be taught as a 'chopping' sign, where the horizontal line 'chops' the dots if this helps the pupils to grasp the concept of subdivision.
- Teach the children to use diagrams and tally marks to reflect the underlying concept that they are working on. How could you represent *24 ÷ 6* as equal sharing? Perhaps you could draw 6 plates and allocate your tally marks to each one in turn until you have used them all up. How could you represent *24 ÷ 6* as repeated subtraction? You could draw a line of 24 tally marks and cross them off in groups of 6.
- Get the pupils to show you their diagrams, this helps you to see what they understand about division.

- Give the pupils plenty of practice in repeated subtraction using real objects or manipulatives and show them how to record the operation. *How many teams of three could we make from our class?*
- Give the pupils plenty of practice in sharing real items out into equal shares. Dealing out playing cards is an easy and practical division exercise. *We have 24 cards and six players, deal the cards out and record the division fact that you found. What if we only had 3 players, how many cards would they each have?*
- Give explicit teaching and demonstration on the relationship between multiplication (repeated addition) and division (repeated subtraction).
- Make sets of multiplication and division facts, with each fact on a different card. Get the children to pair up a multiplication fact with a matching division fact.
- Explore whole numbers and discover their own, unique multiplication and division facts. Encourage the children to make charts of what they find out.
- Show the pupils how they can use a multiplication square to find out division facts.
- Recognise that some children with dyscalculia may have continuing difficulties with the mechanical process of division and the recall of division facts. In this case they should use a calculator so that they can proceed to more interesting applied mathematics.
- Long division is a multi-step process that many pupils find confusing. It should not be introduced until the child either knows their division facts well or can use a number square efficiently. They must also be very comfortable with place value and regrouping and exchanging. Always provide a step-by-step guide for those children who understand the concept but find it hard to remember the sequence of operations.
- Encourage the pupil to use a calculator if they find the mechanics of division difficult to master.

Chapter 19

LEARNING NUMBER FACTS

A profound difficulty in recalling basic number facts is one of the hallmarks of a pupil with dyscalculia. Long after their peers have demonstrated quick and accurate recall, the pupil with dyscalculia may still be laboriously recalculating the same facts over and over again. Years of tedious practice often seem to have little or no effect. The pupil's confidence drops and their attitude towards mathematics becomes increasingly negative.

Knowing number facts is often seen in the same light as being able to spell. It is something that everyone 'ought' to be able to do. And yet we know that there are many capable adults, often very successful in their own spheres, who continue to be poor spellers or who still do not know their tables!

There is a real temptation to hold back those children who do not know their number facts. We may narrow their mathematics curriculum to their areas of deficit, in the hope that sooner or later they will master the number facts. In taking this approach we may restrict the pupils' access to areas of the mathematics curriculum that they could do well in, and consign them to a mathematics programme that frustrates and discourages them.

While it is important to give all pupils the opportunity to learn the basic number facts, we must also keep a sense of perspective. We must carefully budget the amount of effort invested against the observed benefits. If a huge amount of effort has produced negligible benefits then, in future, time and effort might be better invested in developing more promising lines of learning.

Action plans for successful learning

- Provide the technology needed for problem solving. Use calculators and computer spreadsheets to compensate for difficulties in recalling number facts.
- Provide charts, tables and concrete resources to help with number facts.
- Avoid holding a pupil back solely on the basis of their poor retention of number facts.
- Avoid assessing a pupil's competence in mathematics purely on their ability to recall number facts.
- Get the pupils to make their own 'Maths Memo Book' where they can record information they have trouble remembering (number facts, working methods, mnemonics etc).

- Get pupils to keep a personal learning log that records the number facts they *do* know.
- Underpin rote learning with understanding. Avoid mechanical recitation without comprehension.
- Ask: *If this is the answer, what was the question?* to give practice in using number facts.
- Teach a small number of facts at one time. Provide a lot of learning and practice and repeated revision.
- Teach times tables in stages and emphasise the duplication that occurs. Once the children know one table they know several facts for other times tables without further learning being necessary.
- Use empty number charts and get the children to fill in the answers instead of reciting times tables. This helps to overcome the pupil's difficulty in remembering the sequence and reinforces the duplication of facts that occurs. It also helps to develop recall of a specific fact without the need to say the whole table through.
- Emphasise reverses and turnarounds: $\boxed{6 + 7 = 13}$ and $\boxed{7 + 6 = 13}$ $\boxed{5 + 7 = 12}$ and $\boxed{12 - 7 = 5}$
- Teach thinking strategies such as using double and halves.
- Use computer programs that provide an entertaining way of practising number facts.
- Provide interactive and intensive practice with motivational games. There are literally hundreds of games to play.
- Honky Tonky (a number fact recognition game).

The teacher decides whether addition, subtraction, multiplication, division or a mixture of operations is going to be used. Ten to 12 whole numbers are written on the board.

The teacher calls out a number statement such as *5 + 3*. If the answer is on the board the pupils shout it out: *Eight!* If the answer is not on the board the children have to call out *Honky Tonky!*

- Number King (a number fact game).

One person thinks of a number and writes it on a piece of paper that is then folded in two so that the number is hidden. They then answer *yes* or *no* to questions about the mystery number.

The aim of the game is to guess the mystery number. The children may ask questions using addition facts. The game can also be used for subtraction, multiplication or division facts or a mixture of all four operations: *Is it more than 3 + 4? Is it less than 8 + 8?* A running record is kept of the answers on the board so that everyone can keep track.

Yes	No
> 3 + 4	< 4 + 4
< 8 + 8	> 5 + 5
> 6 + 6	

- Times Tables Bingo. Play the Tables Bingo game with a group of children or the whole class. There are two levels of difficulty. Red Tables Bingo covers multiplication tables 1–5 (easy level). Blue Tables Bingo covers multiplication tables 6–12 (more difficult level). For older or more able children you can use both levels together, to cover all the multiplication tables from 1 to 12.

Red Bingo

15	40	33	5	22
30	2	25	9	21
36	24	4	32	20
27	45	55	6	28
35	3	18	48	8
36	16	60	10	15
14	50	12	30	44

Blue Bingo

6	99	8	44	63
16	12	27	56	9
20	22	18	63	70
35	32	10	24	36
88	28	77	90	49
55	50	21	121	72
45	42	30	14	144
84	27	48	100	7
120	80	33	54	55
66	110	81	64	60
72	72	40	108	96

Give each child playing the game a photocopy of the chart of numbers for the game they are playing (Red or Blue Bingo). Ask each pupil to choose six numbers on the chart and to circle these numbers. Alternatively they can be allocated a column or a row of the chart they are using. These are then their target numbers.

Multiplication algorithms are called out, taken from the set of tables being used (tables 1 to 5 for the Blue Bingo, tables 6 to 12 for the Red Bingo). If the pupil has the answer to that algorithm as one of their target numbers then it is crossed off. For example the teacher says *Five times eight* and any pupil who has 40 as a target number crosses it off.

The first pupil to cross off all their target numbers is the winner. The game is an effective teaching tool because it encourages the pupils to look at their target numbers and anticipate the algorithms that they need to complete the game.

MEASUREMENT AND RATIONAL NUMBERS

Mathematics is essentially a practical subject where the concepts and skills that are taught have a direct use in real life. Measurement is one of the most practical applications of mathematical concepts and skills.

Even the least academically talented child will need adequate skills in measurement throughout their life. Those employed in practical or technical areas may have a particular need for good understanding and skills in accurate measurement.

An important element in measurement is an understanding of rational numbers.

Chapter 20

MEASUREMENT

DYSCALCULIA AND MEASUREMENT

Measurement involves the accurate use of the number system, applied to practical situations. For children who have difficulties in conceptualising the number system, measurement may prove to be a particular challenge. The child with dyscalculia may have a poor grasp of the order of magnitude of numbers, and as a result find it very difficult to judge the reasonableness of measurement data that they obtain. They often lack an intuitive sense of number and measurement.

Rocco had been measuring outside using a 15 metre measure. He had measured the playground benches which were arranged on each side of the sand pit. With teacher support he measured one bench and found that it was 2 metres long. He then measured another bench and misread his measure and thought that this second bench was 195 metres long (he looked at the centimetres and read them as metres). He then measured one the side of the sandpit and said that it was 13 metres (he had worked from the wrong end of his measure).

Rocco had not realised that the sandpit sides and the bench lengths would have to be very similar dimensions, and that 13 and 195 meters were unrealistic measurements, given that he knew that one bench was 2 metres long.

Pupils with dyscalculia often have particular difficulties with spatial reasoning. They may find it difficult to recognise symmetry or rotation in designs. This in turn flows through to difficulties in 'seeing' the spatial relationships in linear measuring tasks. Rocco did not 'see' the relationship between the length of the benches and the sides of the sandpit. The sandpit was square but he drew it as an oblong, the benches were all the same length but he drew each separately and did not attempt to match their lengths.

Rocco had also had difficulties in understanding how to read his measuring tape. He took one measurement starting at the wrong end, and did not realise that he was looking at a number line that was in descending order, and that he was tracking from right to left along the measure to get the measurement.

Many pupils with dyscalculia also get muddled with the physical placement and replacement of a ruler or measuring tape. Once again their limitations in basic number sense may make it hard for them to understand that they are essentially working with a number line, but one which is in segments, for example of 20 centimetres, which has to be used and reused to work out longer lengths.

> *Try giving your pupils a measurement problem with unfamiliar units in measurement. For example, can they answer these?*
>
> In another country they measure distances in leagues, instead of miles or kilometres. If a little boy had to walk 2 leagues to school and 2 leagues back again how far would he have to walk each day?
>
> Years ago they used to measure some things in bushels. If a farmer had 2 bushels of wheat and 3 bushels of corn how many bushels of grain did he have altogether?
>
> *You will probably find that some children cannot separate out the units of measurement from the numerical operation. They will object:* I can't do leagues, I don't know how to do bushels.

Many pupils with dyscalculia get very confused with the different units of measurement. They fail to realise that while the units may change the basic numerical operation remains exactly the same.

In linear, mass and liquid measurements the pupil needs to use awareness of base 10 but take it to a new level. So 100 centimetres is renamed as 1 metre, 1000 metres becomes 1 kilometer, 1000 grams is renamed 1 kilogram, 1000 milliltres is renamed 1 litre.

In measurement the numbers are not only renamed but you have alternatives in how to say or record you results. You have counted 130 centimetres. It can either be called 130 centimetres or 1 metre 30cm. You have run 2000 metres or you can call it 2 kilometres.

Regrouping and exchanging in addition and subtraction need to be taught particularly carefully as the data may not be given in a 'user-friendly' form. For example, the question might read: *The cook had 2 kilograms of sugar and used 500 grams for a cake. How much sugar was left over?* This presents a much greater challenge than the same calculation presented as *2000 – 500*, because of course it requires the pupil to 'translate' the 2 kilograms into 2000 grams.

Many forms of measurement also require the pupil to have a good grasp of rational numbers. In real life, measurements are seldom exact and so the pupil will need to understand the concepts and terminology relating to decimals and fractions.

Action plans for successful learning

- Start in the usual way by teaching informal measurement using arbitrary measures such as hands, feet, pencils etc. Emphasise estimation and checking of data against reasonable expectations: *If Sally is 29 pencils tall, how tall do you think Sasha is? Remember Sally is a little bit taller than Sascha.*
- Encourage pupils with poor spatial skills to use language to mediate the task. If Rocco had been able to say, *The benches all look the same length* or *The sandpit is about the same length as the bench*, he would have been less likely to make major measuring errors.
- Give explicit instruction about the use of measuring devices, for example stressing the importance of correct placement when lifting and replacing a measuring device such as a pencil or a ruler.
- Give explicit teaching on using a wide range of names for measuring units so that the pupils learn that the numerical operation is independent of the unit of measurement. It does not matter if you are travelling in miles or kilometres, the numbers are the same.
- Have frequent quick checks on estimated measurements in everyday situations: *How long do you think this new skipping rope is? How much drink can fit in Todd's new drink bottle? How heavy do you think this parcel is?* Record the guesses on the board and then check or measure to see who was the closest.
- Encourage the development of an intuitive sense of measurement by practising estimation. Provide a sample (with a given weight, volume or length) and ask the pupils to estimate the weight, volume or length of another item: *This packet of biscuits weighs 300 grams, how much do you guess this little packet of biscuits weighs? This ribbon is 1 metre long. How long do you think this piece of string is?*
- Get children to weigh, measure and sort to gain familiarity with measures in practical situations such as cooking, craft and construction.
- Have a range of containers that can be filled with liquid. Get the children to sort them into groups such as *less than 1 litre, more than 1 litre, more than 2 litres.*
- Have a selection of pre-packed grocery items and get the children to sort them into weight categories: *less than 100 grams, less than 500 grams, less than 1 kilogram.*

- Have a set of ribbons or ropes to be sorted into named lengths: *less than 10 centimetres, less than 50 centimetres, less than 1 metre.*
- Provide a range of pre-packed grocery items and get the children to make a spreadsheet that gives the product name and the weight or liquid measure given on the container. Tell them to put the items in order of weight or liquid measure. You could also get them to check that the labels were correct by reweighing the packs.
- Have empty grocery containers with the labels removed. Get the pupils to estimate the weights or liquid measures that had been in the containers. Check against identical items that are still full and still have their labels attached.
- Get the children to collect measurement data and use a spreadsheet to collate the information:

Less than 1cm	Between 1 and 10cm	Between 11 and 20cm	Between 21 and 50cm	Between 51 and 100cm	More than 100cm (1 m)
An ant	My pencil	Tom's drink bottle	My atlas	My sports bag	Cord on my anorak
An eyelash		My shoe			

- Have a chart up on the wall to show all the main types of measurement – make sure there is an illustration as well as numbers and words to help children connect. For example, in a chart of liquid measures have a picture of a teaspoon to represent 5 millilitres, and pictures of milk cartons to represent 1 litre and 2 litres.
- Provide explicit teaching in the four operations using measurements, as the regrouping and exchanging requirements are considerably more complex. For example, 1 litre has to be re-written as 1000 millilitres before division can be commenced.

Chapter 21
RATIONAL NUMBERS

DYSCALCULIA AND RATIONAL NUMBERS

Pupils with dyscalculia usually have marked difficulties with the number system. For them, rational numbers may be yet another complexity within an already confusing system.

Before decimals are grasped the pupil must have a clear understanding of the way our number system relates to patterns of ten. Decimals are, of course, simply part of the base 10 system, which fill in the gaps between one whole number and the next. Many pupils believe that there are no numbers at all between one whole number and the next, and so find it very difficult to conceptualise decimals as an intrinsic part of the number line.

This essential concept is often not clearly understood even when the pupil can perform basic operations such as addition and subtraction of decimals. They may well learn the technique and go through the correct working method without being able to say what it all means.

Fractions present the pupil with another type of challenge. In fractions the base is varied, and wholes are not always subdivided into tens. For instance, a whole might be subdivided into thirds so that the child has to adjust to using base 3 as the foundation for working out fractions, while still using base 10 for whole numbers. For pupils who have an insecure grasp of the number system and base 10, this can seem very puzzling indeed.

As with decimals, the pupil also has to understand that in between one whole number and the next there are an infinite range of other numbers, which occupy previously invisible positions on the number line. If children cannot count in fractions and in decimals then they will be much less likely to understand the underlying concepts.

For pupils with spatial reasoning difficulties, fractions and decimals may prove to be particularly difficult. Many children with dyscalculia find it very difficult to visualise fractions or decimals of part of a whole, especially when this is taught using diagrams rather than words.

Pupils with language-related difficulties may also find it hard to sift out the difference between ordinal numbers (third, tenth, sixth etc) and fractions and decimals. This is because they relate the words to rank ordering (*I came third in the race)* and not subdivision (*You've got one-third of the cake).*

The other complication for pupils learning to deal with fractions is that sometimes the fraction relates to a single item such as *one-third of a cake,* while sometimes fractions relate to a group of items such as *one-third of 24.*

Of the two types of fraction presented, the first is easier to grasp. It is quite clearly a subdivision of a single, solid item. As such it is fairly easy to visualise and conceptualise.

The second type (*one-third of 24)* is much harder. The pupil has to visualise a group of single items, and then understand that this group is to be subdivided. It also requires the pupil to perform arithmetic to identify the numerical quantity that results from the subdivision.

Action plans for successful learning

- Make sure that the pupil has a sound grasp of base 10 with whole numbers before attempting to teach decimals or fractions.
- Give explicit teaching so that the pupils understand that while they count in whole numbers, there are numerical positions between each whole number that often need to be taken into account.
- Give plenty of practical counting experience to reinforce the concept that whole numbers are often inadequate to describe the quantities that you are counting. You can use fruit that has been cut up, chalk sticks that are of varying sizes, bottles that are not full etc.
- For example, count apples that have been cut into pieces. You can put them back together but you do not have a whole number of complete apples. Discuss with the children how the number of apples can be described: *six whole apples and two little bits … six whole apples and nearly another whole apple.* Talk about the need for a standardised counting and naming system.
- Practise counting in fractions and decimals to reinforce the concept that these numbers are part of the number line and counting sequence, and use a printed number line to help. For example count *one, one and a half, two, two and a half, three, three and a half, four* or *One point one, one point two, one point three, one point four, etc.*

- Teach decimals as an extension of the base 10 system. There is nothing magical about 'decimals' except that the decimal point tells you that you have moved into a new place value that is smaller than a whole number.
- Teach halves and quarters first as they are the most familiar to children. They are the two fractions that have special names.
- Teach fractions using language instead of diagrams for those pupils who may find spatial reasoning difficult: *If we cut an apple in three we call each piece a third. If we cut an apple in six we call each piece a ...? If we have two of those pieces we can say we have two ...?*
- Use real objects as well as diagrams to teach basic fractions. Clear plastic water bottles work well. Use identical bottles and mark them up with waterproof pens or labels to show the fractions you are teaching. Encourage the children to fill and refill the bottles (with water or dry sand) to explore the fractions and their relationship with a whole.
- Look at citrus fruits: *How many segments in an orange? If there are 12 segments this means that each segment is one-twelfth.* Show the children cards with fractions written on. *Can you read the fraction and show me five twelfths of an orange? How many twelfths in half an orange? Can you show me one-third of the whole orange? How many segments in one-third of an orange?*
- Avoid using circles to illustrate fractions. Many children with dyscalculia are confused by this, because they find it hard to 'see' whether the segments are equal or not. Generally they will find it easier to understand the diagram if it is more pictorial and a regular shape such as a 'brick' or a 'bar'.
- Encourage the children to make their own manipulatives. Provide them with six strips of card or lengths of wood that are all the same length. Show them how to measure and mark so that one strip is marked into two halves, the next strip into four quarters and so on so that they have their own fraction bars for halves, quarters, thirds, fifths and sixths. Get them to colour and mark their own personal manipulatives. Then develop confidence and familiarity by asking *Show me two-thirds, show me one-fifth etc.*

Then develop understanding further by asking the pupils to find equivalent fractions – for example, *two-quarters is the same as one-half* – by using their own personal reference materials.

- Use modelling clay and get the children to make cakes, bananas, snakes or anything that they can cut up into thirds, quarters etc. Some children with dyscalculia will find this a difficult task and may need assistance in 'seeing' what, for example, one third of a cake looks like.

- When teaching fractions of whole numbers, make sure that you start with a very distinct group. For example use 24 Smarties in a packet rather than 24 Smarties loose on the desk. The concept of breaking up a larger group into smaller subgroups is a difficult one for many children. Working with the idea of one-quarter of a packet is much easier than working with the concept of one-quarter of 24.

- Teach pupils how to 'read' fractions. Look under the 'chopping line' (the horizontal line that separates the denominator from the numerator) to find out how many parts the whole was 'chopped' into. Look at the number on the top of the 'chopping line' to see how many of those pieces you have.

- Try to provide manipulatives that emphasise the fact that the decimals that the child is working with are smaller than a whole number. Get the children to make their own manipulatives with modelling clay 'snakes'. Start with one whole and then cut it into ten pieces and mark the pieces with the appropriate decimal.

- Teaching addition and subtraction of fractions with a common denominator can be a challenging and abstract concept. Try Zoo Medicine to make the task more interesting:

The animals in the zoo sometimes get sick and the zoo vet has found that bananas are good medicine. But, as you all know; too much medicine is not a good thing. Too little medicine is not a good thing either. You have to get it just right. In the zoo it is very tricky because the big animals need much more medicine than the little animals. But the zoo vet has worked it out.

The prescription list looks like this:

Elephants: 3 bananas after breakfast, lunch and dinner each day.

Mountain goats: 1½ bananas after breakfast, lunch and dinner each day.

Wombats: ½ a banana after breakfast, lunch and dinner each day.

Monkeys: ⅓ banana after breakfast, lunch and dinner each day.

Rabbits: ¼ banana after breakfast, lunch and dinner each day.

Obviously as the teacher you can vary the list to suit the fractions that you are teaching. Get the children to work out various prescriptions: How many bananas will the rabbit need if she is sick for three days? How many bananas will the wombat need if he is sick for seven days? *You may need to provide diagrams of the bananas cut into their fractions to allow the children to count and calculate the answers. You can extend this to include calculations that involve fractions with different denominators as part of your teaching if you wish.*

TEACHER RESOURCES

SECTION

6

PARENT INFORMATION SHEET: AT HOME WITH MATHS

Mathematics is a very important part of your child's schooling. Being able to enjoy maths and succeed in the subject can make a lot of difference to your child's confidence at school.

One of the best ways you can help your child to succeed in maths is to make sure that they feel really at home with numbers in everyday situations.

YOUNGER CHILDREN

- Find stories, puzzles and rhymes that involve counting and written numbers.
- Let your child hear you count aloud as you cook, garden or shop.
- As you go about your neighbourhood encourage your child to notice printed numbers. Point out and count the numbers on the gates as you pass by. Show them the numbers on your bus ticket or on your receipt and explain what the numbers mean.
- Count with your child: *How many bears in the pram? How many steps to the gate? How many socks in the drawer?*
- Use words such as *Which is the biggest? Are there enough? How many left?* In order to draw your child into thinking mathematically.
- One of the most important concepts in maths is that of 'composition' (understanding that one number can be composed of two or more other numbers). Show your child this concept in everyday life: *We've got 5 cakes, 2 chocolate, 2 strawberry and 1 vanilla. Tomorrow there will be 2 boys and 2 girls, that's 4 children altogether. We used to have 6 picnic chairs but 2 are broken so now we only have 4.*

OLDER CHILDREN

- Enjoy numbers when you watch sport. Talk to your child about the scores, the records and the league tables. Sport provides excellent opportunities for mathematical talking and thinking. Encourage your child to look at the sports section in the newspaper for the final scores, records times etc.

- Encourage your child to get used to handling money as soon as possible, so that they begin to get real life experience of adding, subtracting, multiplying and dividing with money.
- Teach your child to be a serious shopper and to look at prices, weights, measures etc to find the best buy.
- Open a bank account for your child and show them how to read their statement and check their deposits and withdrawals.
- Encourage older children to use a computer spreadsheet to compile a summary of their school grades or sports scores or an inventory of their hobby collection.
- Encourage your child to count in 2s, 5s and 20s when counting large numbers.
- Encourage your child to use numbers that are already provided on packets, containers etc: *How many paper clips in that pack? So will one pack be enough? How much elastic on that card?*
- Involve your child in practical activities such as cooking, household projects, repairs and gardening so that weighing, measuring, calculating, counting, budgeting and timing all become part of everyday life.
- Encourage craft and construction activities, both really help to promote good mathematical thinking.
- Try to use decimals, fractions and percentages when you can: *We've only got about one third of those labels left. You save up 75% and I'll give you the other 25% of the price of the bike. Its about 1.6 metres long.*
- Show your child how you use estimation and rounding to work out the maths that you need. You probably use estimation more often than 'proper' maths when you buy materials for a project at home or in the garden, or work out your budget or check your supermarket bill. Include your child when you do this type of maths: *Let's say it will be about £3.00 each to get in, and maybe another £1.50 for lunch for the 4 of us, so say £4.50. Better make that £5.00 to be on the safe side. Four of us at £5.00 each, so £20.00 should be fine.*
- Extend your child's knowledge of numbers by showing them bigger numbers and talking about them. Look at expensive items such as skateboards, computers, bikes, cars etc to increase your child's familiarity with large numbers.
- Promote your child's mental arithmetic and memory for number facts by playing family games where scores have to be kept and added up.
- Talk to your child's teacher about the methods that are used in school and the terminology being used, so that if you help your child with school maths you are working along the same lines as the teacher and not confusing your child.

- Encourage your child to make intelligent use of a calculator. Show them how to check their answer against an estimate of the right answer.
- Use your family tree and family history to give your child a sense of time: *Gran was 60 when you were born and Great Uncle Charlie is 10 years older than Gran.*
- Use a calendar or yearly planner for your family organisation. Put it somewhere where everyone can see it and use it to mark in important dates.

Teachers may copy this handout to give to parents.

PARENT INFORMATION SHEET: MATHS ON THE MOVE

Did you know that you can turn the car, bus, train or ferry into a great maths classroom for your children?

Maths is not just about 'doing sums'. Maths is about thinking mathematically, seeing numbers around you, and understanding what those numbers mean.

LOOK OUT OF THE CAR WINDOW

- Is the car ahead a higher or lower number than you?
- What is the highest number car you see today?
- What is the lowest number car you see today?
- What is the smallest and biggest number you could possibly have?
- Add all the digits in the car number plates you see – which has the biggest number?
- What patterns can you see in the numbers on the cars around you?

Patterns might include: 246 (sequence of even numbers)
         579 (sequence of odd numbers)
         257 (2 + 5 = 7)
         236 (2 × 3 = 6)
         826 (8 − 2 = 6)

- What numbers can you see on the large vehicles around you? What do the numbers mean? (You might see the company's telephone number, the weight limitations, the engine size, the number of passengers it can carry, its model number etc).

LOOK INSIDE THE CAR

- Look at the displays on the dash. What do all the different numbers mean?
- Watch how the display changes as you travel, see how the numbers change 3794.7, 3794.8, 3794.9, 3795.0, 3795.1.
- How far has this car travelled altogether? How far has the car travelled each year?

- How much fuel do we have? Is the gauge full, half full, quarter empty?
- What does the manual say about how far we can drive once we have reached 'red' on the fuel gauge?
- What does the manual say about how much fuel we can put in the car?
- How much would this cost us?
- About how far could we travel on a full tank?
- Do we have a car licence? When does it run out?
- What does the car manual tell us about tyre pressures?
- What is the maximum weight the car can carry or tow?
- How often do the windscreen washers wipe the screen in one minute?

DISTANCES & MAPS

- Look at the distances on road signs.
- Set the distance trip to 0 and see how far you travel on a journey.
- Time how long your journey took.
- Estimate how far you travel in a week, a month or a year.
- Look at the map, where are we now?
- Use the index to look up your street. Use the page and grid reference to find it on the map.
- Find your school by page and grid reference. Can you see the route you usually take? Is there another route?
- Can you see the distances shown on the map?
- What does the square grid mean? Can you find the key that tells you?
- Are all the maps in your road atlas the same? Are some on a different scale?

STOPPED ON RED

- How many cars go past in the other direction before the lights change?
- What is the most common colour for a car?
- On average how many people in each car?
- What position are we at the lights? First? Third? Tenth?
- How long do the lights stay red?

ROAD SIGNS

- Look at the speed limits and compare them with your speed.
- Are the lights mostly red or mostly green as you drive your route?

- Look for road signs that tell you how far to go until the next junction or exit or turn-off.
- Look for road signs that tell you about gradients or slope.
- Look for road signs that tell you about height or weight limitations.
- Look for signs on buildings that tell you the date, the temperature or any other information.
- What are the speed limits in town? On the motorway? Near a school? In the car park?
- Look at the prices for fuel as you pass by the filling stations. Which is the cheapest?
- Look at any ferry, bridge or toll way. How much for a car? How much for a motor cycle?

PARKING

- How many cars are parked altogether in this car park?
- Look at the parking restrictions. How long can we stay? When can we park?
- Look at parking fees. How much to stay one hour? Two hours?
- How long can you stay in the car park if you only have £3.00 change?
- What coins can you use to pay for the parking?

ON THE BUS, TRAIN, TRAM OR FERRY

- Look at the timetable and work out when your transport is due.
- Look at the fares. What is the cheapest way to travel to your destination?
- Look at the route on a map to see where the bus etc comes from and goes to.
- Look at where you could change to another type of transport.
- Look at the display board and talk about the information that it gives.
- Look at your ticket, what do the numbers on it mean?

Teachers may copy this handout to give to parents.

PARENT INFORMATION SHEET: AT HOME WITH TELLING THE TIME

It will really help your child succeed with telling the time if you can make sure that they feel at home with using time in everyday situations.

- Even with a very young child, use time as part of your everyday conversation: *Soon, only about five minutes to wait now* or *It's a long time to wait, four or five hours maybe.*
- Quite a few children do not realise that the hands of a clock or the digital numbers do actually move! Stand with your child and watch it happen.
- Give your child a sense of your own family timetable: *We get up at 7 o'clock ... Mum has to leave for work by 8.15 ... School starts at 9 o'clock ... we get home at 4 o'clock ... we were late today because of sports practice ... bedtime is usually 7.30 on school days and about 8.30 on weekends.*
- When your child is waiting for something encourage them to use the clock: *When the big hand reaches round to the 12, and the little hand is on the 6, then it will be 6 o'clock and it will be time for your TV programme. When the clock says 06.00 then we will know it is time to turn the TV on.*
- Count down the time to an exciting event: *Grandma should be here in less than three hours. Only five minutes and it will be ready to get out of the oven.*
- Show your child how time can be found not only on clocks on the wall at home, but also on your watch, computer screen, mobile phone, car instruments and home equipment such as the television.
- Point out how the time is often shown on big display clocks, or in digital displays in lifts, car parks in your local shopping area etc.
- Explain how time can be expressed in different ways: *That's a digital clock, 2.45 is the just the same as quarter to three, you can say 'Two forty five' or you can say 'Quarter to three', it means the same thing.*
- *Your photos ready in one hour. Prescriptions ready in 30 minutes. Back in 10 mins:* involve your child in working out when to go back.
- Opening and closing times of shops, banks, exhibitions etc are usually displayed prominently. Get your child to check them out for you.
- Get your child to look up the times of their favourite TV programmes in the TV guide.

- Look at the playing times on videos or DVDs *'How long does it take to play? If we start it now will we have time to see the end?*
- Look in the newspaper and get your child to check the times of the film that you want to see.
- Car parking is a good opportunity for talking about time: *How much will it cost for 2 hours? How long do we need? We've only got one hour on this spot, it is ten past two now so when will we have to be back?*
- Look at the car parking receipt that you got as you drove out of the car park. Does it show the time you went in? Does it show the time you went out?
- Look at directions on packets, and encourage your child to understand and use the instructions relating to time: *Microwave on high for 2 mins.*
- Cook with your child and encourage them to follow the instructions: *Cook for 10 minutes on each side.*
- Get your child to help you calculate cooking times: *15 minutes per kilo + an extra 10 minutes.*
- Allow your child to play with the kitchen timer, so that they get a sense of how time passes, and what a time span such as 5 minutes actually 'feels' like.
- Show them how to set the alarm clock or automatic timer.
- Encourage your child to use the electronic time display on your microwave, washing machine or dishwasher: *Are the vegetables nearly done? How long before that washing is finished?*
- Show your child how to check the time by using the talking clock on the phone.
- Talk to your child about different time zones across the world. Explain to them how when you are just getting up, somewhere, on the opposite side of the world, children are just going to bed.
- Find a world clock on your computer, so that child can look up the current time in various cities for themselves.
- Watching sports is a great way to introduce your child to the concept of time. Many team sports are time limited, with definite divisions such as *half time, quarter time, full time* .
- Talk to your child about the starting time for the game and how long each half or quarter is going to be. Keep track of the time, 5 minutes before the final whistle can be a very exciting time in the match!
- Organise your own family sports, with distances run and time taken recorded by your child.
- Encourage your child to try for their 'personal best' times in running, swimming etc.
- Follow sporting events through radio, television or newspapers. Take an interest in world record times, personal best times, winning times etc (this is also great for

introducing your child to the concept of decimals and the importance of very small shifts in numbers).

• Before a journey, encourage your child to look at the time schedule. Talk to them about what time you need to leave home to arrive at the right time. Show them how to judge time, leaving yourself a margin for error: *The bus leaves at 3 o'clock, so if we leave at 2.45 that gives us 15 minutes, it only takes 10 minutes to walk there, so we should be in good time.*

• Encourage your child to look at timetables so that they understand how departure and arrival times are set out.

• Call into the local train station, airport or bus depot, and look at the display boards with your child, so that they can see how information about times of services are displayed.

• If you have timed telephone calls, show your child how calls are billed.

• Play time estimation games with your child. Let somebody run the stop watch and guess how long 2 minutes is. Try guessing other times such as 5 minutes, 10 minutes, an hour. Who was the closest?

Teachers may copy this handout to give to parents.

PUPIL QUESTIONNAIRE:
WHAT I THINK ABOUT MATHS

Just circle YES or NO. There are no right or wrong answers.

I really like maths	YES NO
Some of the maths we do at school is too hard for me	YES NO
My friends like to do maths	YES NO
Maths is often very hard to understand	YES NO
Maths is good fun	YES NO
I am good at maths	YES NO
I will use maths a lot when I am older	YES NO
Maths is usually boring	YES NO
I feel happy when the teacher says it's time for maths	YES NO
I wish that we did harder maths in school	YES NO
Sometimes I tell my family about the maths we do at school	YES NO
I understand the maths we do at school	YES NO
Sometimes I make up my own maths to do for fun	YES NO
Maths is very useful to me	YES NO
Teachers think that you should do the maths without any help	YES NO
I think that maths is interesting	YES NO
Sometimes I ask my parents to give me some maths to do	YES NO
Sometimes I feel a bit scared to ask for help in maths	YES NO
My parents think that I should be better at maths	YES NO
Other kids at school think it is OK to like maths	YES NO
I sometimes get really confused in maths	YES NO
I wish we did more maths in school	YES NO
I sometimes feel worried about maths	YES NO
I am OK about asking the teacher for help	YES NO

Note to teachers: You can photocopy this questionnaire as often as you like. Remind your pupils that there are no right or wrong answers. They should put down what they really think. The pupils can be anonymous or you can ask them to put their name on their sheet.

YOUR CHILD AND MATHS: PARENT QUESTIONNAIRE

Dear parent, as teachers we it would help us to know what you think about your child and maths. Just tick the items that you agree with.

Your child's name: ……………………………………………………..

I think that my child usually finds maths

very easy ☐ usually OK ☐ quite difficult ☐ very difficult ☐

☐ My child seems to enjoy maths

☐ Sometimes my child gets upset and anxious when doing maths

☐ I think my child is reasonably confident with maths

☐ Sometimes my child gets angry doing maths

☐ I think my child expects maths to be too difficult and gives up

☐ Maths homework often stresses our family out

☐ My child often asks me for help with maths

☐ Sometimes I am not sure how to help my child with maths

☐ I feel anxious about my child's progress in maths

☐ I think that my child tries to avoid doing maths

☐ My child seems to cope with the maths homework without assistance

☐ We spend extra time helping our child with maths

☐ We sometimes buy maths workbooks or make up maths at home to give extra practice

☐ We send our child to maths coaching because we feel that extra help is needed

☐ I am confident that my child understands what to do in maths

☐ I think that maths is a difficult subject for most children

☐ I would like to learn more about how to help my child with maths.

REFERENCES AND BIBLIOGRAPHY

Anderson, J.R., Reder, L.M. and Simon, H.A. (1996) 'Situated learning and Education.' *Educational Researcher,* 25,4, pp. 5–96.

Black, J.E., Isaacs, B.J., Anderson, A.A. and Alcantara, W.T. (1990) 'Learning causes synaptogenesis, whereas motor activity causes angiogenesis in the cerebral cortex of adult rats.' *Proceedings of the National Academy of Sciences USA,* 87, pp. 5568–72.

Butterworth, B. and Yeo, D. (2004) *Dyscalculia Guidance.* NferNelson, London.

Canfield, R.L. and Smith, E.G. (1996) Number based expectations and sequential enumeration by 5 month old infants. *Developmental Psychology,* 32, pp. 269–79.

DfES (2001) *Guidance to Support Pupils with Dyslexia and Dyscalculia.* DfES circular.

Gardner, H. (1993) *Multiple intelligences: The theory in practice.* Basic books, London.

Garnett, K. (1998) 'Math Learning Disabilities.' *Learning Disabilities Journal of CEC.* www.ldonline.org, accessed July 2004.

Gathercole, S.E. and Pickering, S.J. (2000) 'Working memory deficitsi in children with low achievements in the national curriculum at 7 years of age.' *Journal of Educational Psychology,* 70, pp. 177–94.

Geary, D.C., Hamson, C.O. and Hoard, M.K.(2000) 'Numerical and arithmetic cognition: a longitudinal study of process and concept deficits in pupils with learning disability.' *Journal of Experimental Pupil Psychology,* 77, pp. 236–63.

Geary, D.C. (2004) 'Mathematics and learning disabilities.' *Journal of Learning Disabilities,* 37, pp. 4–15.

Gersten, R. (1999) 'Number Sense: Rethinking Instruction for Pupils Mathematical Disabilities.' *Journal of Special Education,* 0512/2001. Lazear, D. (1991). *Seven ways of knowing: Understanding multiple intelligences.* Palitine: Skylight.

Levine, M. (2002) *Misunderstood Minds* (web and video materials). WGBH, Boston.

Mehler, J. and Christophe, A. (1995) *Maturation and learning in the first year of life in the Cognitive Neurosciences.* MIT Press, Cambridge MA.

National Centre for Learning Disabilities (2004) *Fact Sheet: Dyscalculia.* www.ldonline.org, accessed July 2004.

National Research Council (2000) *How people learn. Brain, mind, experience and school.* National Academy Press, Washington.

Nolte, J. (1988) *The Human Brain.* The C.V. Mosby Company, St Louis.

Shalev, R.S. and Gross-Tur, V. (2001) 'Developmental Dyscalculia.' *Pediatric Neurology,* 24, pp. 337–42.

Starkey, P.E.S. and Gelman, R. (1990) 'Numerical Abstraction by human infants.' *Cognition*, 36, pp. 97–127.

Willis, S. (1990) *Being Numerate: What Counts?* ACER, Melbourne.

Wilson, K.M. and Swanson, H.L. (2001) 'Are mathematics disabilities due to a domain-general or a domain-specific working memory deficit?' *Journal of Learning Disabilities*, 34, pp. 237–48.

Printed in the United Kingdom
by Lightning Source UK Ltd.
135790UK00009B/11-18/A